MARK TWAIN'S
HUCKLEBERRY FINN

RACE, CLASS AND SOCIETY

TEXT AND CONTEXT

Editors

ARNOLD KETTLE
Professor of Literature
Open University

and

A. K. THORLBY
Professor of Comparative Literature
University of Sussex

◆

MICHAEL EGAN
Mark Twain's Huckleberry Finn:
Race, Class and Society

BERNARD HARRISON
Henry Fielding's Tom Jones:
The Novelist as Moral Philosopher

JEREMY HAWTHORN
Virginia Woolf's Mrs. Dalloway:
A Study in Alienation

DOUGLAS JEFFERSON
Jane Austen's Emma:
A Landmark in English Fiction

LAURENCE LERNER
Thomas Hardy's The Mayor of Casterbridge:
Tragedy or Social History?

Other Titles in Preparation

'7

'03

4

6

MARK TWAIN'S
Huckleberry Finn

RACE, CLASS AND SOCIETY

Michael Egan

SUSSEX UNIVERSITY PRESS

1977

Published for

SUSSEX UNIVERSITY PRESS

by

Chatto & Windus Ltd
40 William IV Street
London WC2N 4DF

*

Clarke, Irwin & Co Ltd
Toronto

For

Luke and Daniel

Hardback ISBN 0 85621 060 9

Paperback ISBN 0 85621 061 7

©Michael Egan 1977

Printed Offset Litho in Great Britain by
Cox & Wyman Ltd,
London, Fakenham and Reading

CONTENTS

7 - 65

ACKNOWLEDGEMENTS

I would like to thank Professor Everett Emerson, of the English Department, University of Massachusetts at Amherst, and Professor Arnold Kettle of the Open University, for their help in preparing this study. Professor Anthony Thorlby of Sussex University read the final draft and made a large number of valuable suggestions which were incorporated.

More generally, I want to thank my students who in ways large and small have helped shape my attitude to Mark Twain.

Michael Egan

PART ONE

Structure and Audience

1

Introduction

For all its reputation for light and sparkle, S.L. Clemens' *Adventures of Huckleberry Finn* (1885) is one of the darkest novels in American fiction. It seems necessary to make this point at the outset since it is a work that has been both absurdly overpraised and undervalued. As recently as 1957, for example, the Board of Education in New York City banned the book from elementary and junior high schools because Huck, speaking the language of his culture and circumstances, uses the word 'nigger'. But this was only the latest move by public authorities to keep this 'juveniles' book' from corrupting the young. When the novel appeared in America in February, 1885, most reviewers either ignored it or attacked it savagely on the grounds of its unsuitability for children. The *Boston Advertiser* condemned Twain for his irreverence and judged his book a failure; the *Boston Transcript* declared the story to be 'so flat, as well as coarse, that nobody wants to read it after a taste of it'; and an anonymous reviewer in *Life*, afterwards identified as Robert Bridges, a future editor of *Scribner's Magazine*, sarcastically commended the book for children because of its bloodiness and impropriety. Within a month of its publication the *Boston Transcript* reported:

> The Concord (Mass.) Public Library Committee has decided to exclude Mark Twain's latest book from the library. One member of the committee says that, while he does not wish to call it immoral, he thinks it contains but little humor, and that of a very coarse type. He regards it as the veriest trash. The librarian and the other members of the committee entertain similar views, characterising it as rough, coarse, and inelegant, dealing with a series of experiences not elevating, the whole

7

book being more suited to the slums than to intelligent, respectable people.

The *Springfield Republican* applauded this act, adding for good measure the opinion that the moral level of Twain's books was 'low' and 'their perusal cannot be anything less than harmful.' Twain was perversely delighted. In *Huckleberry Finn*, when the king and the duke draw up their handbill announcing the 'Thrilling Tragedy of the King's Camelopard or the Royal Nonesuch!!!' they add at the bottom: 'LADIES AND CHILDREN NOT ADMITTED.' The duke's cynical comment is: 'There. . . if that line don't fetch them, I don't know Arkansaw!' and Twain knew his Massachusetts. The next day he wrote to his publisher, Charles L. Webster: 'The Committee of the Public Library of Concord, Mass., have given us a rattling tip-top puff which will go into every paper in the country. They have expelled Huck from their library as "trash & suitable only for the slums". That will sell 25,000 copies for us, sure.' Still, as Twain's slightly false exuberance indicated, the ban obviously rankled, and when in March he was invited to join the Concord Free Trade Club he agreed, but added rather sourly (under the cloak of a jest) that the town's librarian should know that his action had served only to double the sales of the book.

There was, however, one further curious circumstance which added to the novel's reputation for immorality. Featured in the first edition were one hundred and seventy-four engravings produced by E.W. Kemble, all of which were checked by Twain himself. In November, 1884, however, when the final printing was already in progress, it was discovered that the illustration on page 283 was obscene. Entitled 'Who do you reckon it is?' the cutting portrayed Uncle Silas Phelps, his hips thrust forward and flanked by a grinning Aunt Sally looking sidelong at him, with a disconcertingly erect penis of Lysistratic proportions. Of course the print-run was stopped and publication delayed until the engraving was corrected. Nevertheless the book received pre-publication publicity of dubious value, some of it of a pruriently ambiguous nature. The *New York World*, for instance, lamented Twain's 'dilema' (sic) in a front-page story, and referred sadly to the impending 'most unkindest cut of all.'

Huckleberry Finn thus began its life in a general aura of

8

impropriety, and this may account for its repeated exclusions from the children's shelves of public libraries. Denver and Omaha banned it in 1902 and in 1905 it was removed from the Brooklyn Public Library. Two years later E.L. Pearson, writing in the *Library Journal* (July, 1907), reported in an article called 'The Children's Librarian versus *Huckleberry Finn*' that both it and *Tom Sawyer* had been excluded from some library 'every year' since the word had got about 'that these two books are to be condemned'. These reactions need not be taken too seriously, however. They were the ritualistic reception accorded virtually every major literary work in the late nineteenth century and reflected both the intellectual insecurity and petty-bourgeois prejudices of New England in this period.[1]

On the other hand, of course, *Huckleberry Finn* has been more lavishly exalted than any other novel in American literary history. Ever since Brander Matthews and Thomas Sergeant Perry acclaimed the book on its appearance in 1885, the best critics in each generation have spoken strongly for it. W.D. Howells, Mark Twain's mentor, in 1901 had 'half a mind to give my whole heart to *Huckleberry Finn*. . . I who like *The Connecticut Yankee in King Arthur's Court* so much.' Later T.S. Eliot and Lionel Trilling defended it against the wave of criticism that took its impetus from Van Wyk Brooks' *The Ordeal of Mark Twain* (1920), and F.R. Leavis called it 'supremely the American classic. . . one of the great books of the world.' Creative writers no less than professional critics have been fulsome in their enthusiasm. William Faulkner acknowledged a filial debt; and of course there is Ernest Hemingway's endlessly quoted aphoristic throwaway, in *Green Hills of Africa*, that American fiction begins with it. However, this kind of remark is useful only as a discussion point; in my judgement Hemingway's careless words have harmed the novel more than helped it. A more perceptive comment is Ralph Ellison's: 'I could imagine myself as Huck Finn. . . but not, though I racially identified with him, as Nigger Jim, who struck me as a white man's inadequate portrait of a slave.' As we shall see, this remark comes close to the novel's central critical problem.

I said earlier that *Huckleberry Finn* was a dark-toned work,

[1] For a longer discussion of the prejudices and mentality of late-Victorian New England see the Introduction to my *Ibsen*: *The Critical Heritage* (London: Routledge, 1972) pp. 25–37.

picaresque?

meaning this in two important senses. First, its concerns are far grimmer than is conventionally acknowledged, even by its enthusiasts; and secondly, its intellectual somberness is supported by images of gloom and midnight so persistent they must be accounted deliberate and thematic. It will be important to establish both points unambiguously, for they bear directly on the question of the novel's unity and tight construction. This will in turn affect our reading of it. The circumstances of its composition, scrupulously examined in the 1940s by Bernard DeVoto, and its obvious similarities with the picaresque tradition, have led many commentators into mistaking its episodic nature for fragmentariness. However, as Walter Blair discovered:

> Though Twain finished the manuscript late in August, 1883, he did not send it off until the third week of April, 1884. During more than seven months. . . he apparently revised the partly-typed partly-holograph manuscript thoroughly. This guess is justified by the holograph, about three-fifths of the novel, in the Buffalo Public Library. It shows that not only did he make many revisions while writing, he also made three later revisions. Numerous changes also were made − some doubtless by Howells − between manuscript and book. About a thousand changes testify that he revised with great care. Nor do these tell the whole story. Handwriting, cancellations and pagination show that many pages were inserted and many passages rewritten.
>
> (*Mark Twain and Huck Finn*, California 1960, p. 351.)

Huckleberry Finn was begun in June or July, 1876, as a sequel to *Tom Sawyer* which had been published in the preceding year, and, as Blair points out, it was completed in 1883. This seven-year period of composition was more formal than real, however, since it was substantially written at two major sittings at Twain's summer home in Elmira, New York, the first in 1876 and the second in 1883. If the novel is thus less than superficially picaresque (the Mississippi as highway), this has little to do with Twain's adding piecemeal to the plot over the years. In fact, establishing *Huckleberry Finn* in a tradition with *Tom Jones* only obscures its deeper construction. If one must align it with a European literary genre the epistolary novel would do better, since it illuminates Huck's direct form of address ('the end, your truly,

10

Huck Finn.') and reminds us that Twain originally wrote the whole thing as a single unit, accepting chapter divisions at Webster's behest only after it was completed.

Twain's first sitting yielded about four hundred pages of manuscript, but he was not very satisfied with what he had written. He liked it, he said, 'only tolerably well,' adding that he might 'pigeonhole or burn the MS' when he had finished. Twain's difficulty was that what had started as a genial adventure story for boys was turning into 'Huck Finn's Autobiography', that is, Twain's own, with increasingly serious overtones. I mean by this of course not that the young Sam Clemens ever lit out for the Territory with a runaway slave − though he did leave the Confederate Army during the Civil War and make his way West. My point is that as he wrote he found himself forced for the first time to come to terms with his Southern boyhood. Bernard De Voto was thus both profoundly right and wrong when he said that all Twain's fiction was 'about the society in which his boyhood had been spent. . . with little alteration.' (*Mark Twain in Eruption*, New York, 1940, p. xvii.) In his earlier work, *Tom Sawyer* for example, Twain's conscious folksiness and fatal drive for melodrama had allowed the issue to be evaded; but *Huckleberry Finn* forced him to draw on his most intense memories and experiences. That is one of the reasons why this book and *A Connecticut Yankee in King Arthur's Court*, which followed it, are his two supreme fictions. Towards the end of his career, Twain wrote in *Following the Equator* (1897): 'All that goes to make the *me* in me was in a Missourian village, on the other side of the globe.' He might have added that it was writing *Huckleberry Finn* which had brought him to this truth.

In 1890, in a letter to an unidentified correspondent, he had this to say:

Your surmise is correct, sharply and exactly so − that I confine myself to life with which I am familiar, when pretending to portray life. But I confined myself to the boy life out on the Mississippi because that had a peculiar charm for me and not because I was not familiar with other phases of life. . . . *Now* then: as the most valuable capital, or culture, or education usable in the building of novels is personal experience, I ought to be well equipped for that trade. I surely have the

11

equipment, a wide culture and all of it real, for I don't know anything about books.

Twain then added the following postcript, which he crossed out:

And yet I can't go away from the boyhood period & write novels because *capital* is not sufficient by itself & I lack the other essential: interest in handling the men and experiences of later times.

(DeVoto (ed): *The Portable Mark Twain*, New York, 1946, pp. 9, 773–5.)

This remarkable statement reveals not only the self-consciousness with which Twain relied on the first-hand experiences of his boyhood – 'the most valuable. . . education usable in the building of novels is personal experience' – but the sharpness of his understanding that what passed for fiction in his work was deeply autobiographical. Thus his extraordinary observation, 'I can't. . . write novels,' a confession as movingly perceptive as Michelangelo's, 'I am not a painter.' The parallels are even more striking, for just as Michelangelo was driven to the rediscovery of his true form by the experience of painting the Sistine Chapel, arguably his single greatest achievement, so Twain attempted nothing significant in fiction after completing *Huckleberry Finn* and *A Connecticut Yankee* (1889). This may be partly accounted for by his struggle against bankruptcy; but then so may his later attempts to revive Huck and Tom in trivial further adventures. What Twain genuinely achieved after 1890 was autobiography. His insight was that his true subject had always and only been: himself. 'I confined myself to the boy-life out on the Mississippi. . . not because I was not familiar with other phases of life. . . [but because] I lack the other essential: interest in handling the men and experiences of later times.'

As Twain worked on *Huckleberry Finn* at Elmira in 1876 he discovered that he was, rather disconcertingly, being drawn into a consideration of more complicated issues than he had intended. Huck's journey was plunging him into the heart of the South. The unevenness of the first sixteen chapters (where the narrative was broken off) bears all the marks of a novelistic conception undergoing change. On the other hand, as we will see, Twain's fiction was keeping pace with his evolving political perspectives.

12

Clearly, Twain began with the intention of producing a new adventure story following logically on the heels of *Tom Sawyer*. 'You don't know about me, without you have read a book by the name of *The Adventures of Tom Sawyer*, but that ain't no matter.' Even when the metamorphosed novel finally appeared it was subtitled parenthetically 'Tom Sawyer's Comrade,' and Twain frequently considered publishing the two as companion volumes. Further, there is evidence that the first chapters had originally been written for the final part of the earlier work, but were discarded. As Twain's plot developed, however, with the fleshing out of Huck's personality, with the creation of Pap and the recreation of Jim, so the detail and texture of the antebullum South (together with an increasingly radical perspective) began to be worked into the whole.

I spoke of the recreation of Jim. What I mean is that the eye-rolling darky we encounter in chapter two has nothing in common with the dignified and often complex figure of chapters eight to fifteen. Twain was only partially truthful when he noted in his *Autobiography*:

> We had a faithful and affectionate good friend, ally, and adviser in 'Uncle Dan'l,' a middle-aged slave whose head was the best one in the negro quarter, whose sympathies were wide and warm, and whose heart was honest and simple and knew no guile. He has served me well these many, many years. I have not seen him for more than half a century, and yet spiritually I have had his welcome company a good part of that time, and have staged him in books under his own name and as 'Jim,' and carted him all around. . .
>
> (*Mark Twain's Autobiography*, New York, 1924, p. 100.)

The Jim of chapter two, and of the late, evasion chapters, is not this man. He is a caricature and a travesty, the sort of Jolsonesque mockery Ellison was complaining about. Assuredly he is there in Twain's patronising remark that Uncle Dan'l had the best head 'in the negro quarter', and that, spiritually, Twain has continued to think of him as master to servant ('he has served me well these many, many years'). But it is only in the mature, mid-section of the novel that Jim actually comes to life and begins to beat with the pulses of a real man. The difference indicates Twain's deepening interest in the serious possibilities of his book.

13

At the end of the summer of 1876 Twain put his novel temporarily aside. He was subsequently to remove from what became
chapter twelve the so-called 'raftsman's passage', and replace it
with the sequence aboard the *Walter Scott*. His reasons appear to
have been those of expedience and art: *Huck* was too long,
relative to *Tom Sawyer*, and Twain wished to symbolise his
critique of the corrosive qualities of what he called 'Sir Walter's
disease', the childish courtly romanticism which had, in his judgment, led the South to war and ruin. Further, the excised passage
fitted well enough into *Life on the Mississippi*, which was
published in 1883. As we will see, however, his judgment may
have been more unconsciously directed than he realised. At all
events, with some final additions and corrections to chapters
thirteen and fourteen, this appears to have been the extent of his
modifications to the novel's first third. In the story Cairo has
been missed in the fog and the pair's raft smashed by the culpably
blind river steamer.

Many critics believe that at this juncture Twain was in doubt
concerning his next step, and had decided to await further inspiration. And until quite recently critical orthodoxy, strongly
supported by Bernard DeVoto's pioneering *Mark Twain at Work*
(1942), held that the novel was not resumed for another six
years, that is, until late 1882, after Twain had 'filled up the tank'
of his depleted inspiration with the waters of his visit to the Mississippi valley in that year. But it seems to me Twain knew very
well where his novel was going, and paused more from a sense of
care than perplexity. He was about to undertake a serious and, as
it proved, incisive analysis of the antebellum South, the world of
his boyhood and youth, and he needed time to consider his final
verdict. Unquestionably he foresaw the necessity of a Southern
revisit – *Huckleberry Finn* had become a complicated exercise
– but his work on the novel did not hang upon it. His planned
trip, as he anticipated, would only confirm and clarify details,
not add important new elements to the plot.

For instance, while preparing for the journey in 1882 he
reminded himself: 'Stop at Cairo, Hickman or New Madrid (1
hour) and ask about old feuds.' And indeed he did, though the
parenthetic '1 hour' indicates the weight he attached to it. A talk
with a river pilot elicited the names of two feuding families, the
Darnells and the Watsons, and contributed the small detail,

14

subsequently included in *Huckleberry Finn*, that they lived on opposite sides of the river.

Twain's notes also included the striking recollection that the contending families regularly worshipped the same Christ in the same church – but did so armed to the teeth. Huck makes a similar observation about the Grangerfords and Shepherdsons, with some characteristically heavy irony:

> Next Sunday we all went to church, about three mile, everybody a-horseback. The men took their guns along, so did Buck, and kept them between their knees or stood them handy against the wall. The Shepherdson's done the same. It was pretty ornery preaching – all about brotherly love, and suchlike tiresomeness; but every body said it was a good sermon, and they all talked it over going home, and had such a powerful lot to say about faith and good works, and free grace, and preforeordestination, and I don't know what all, that it did seem to me to be one of the roughest Sundays I had run across yet.
>
> (*Huckleberry Finn*, Chapter 18.)

Finally, and most substantially for the novel, Twain recorded the following, clearly verbatim: 'Once a boy 12 years old connected with the Kentucky family was riding thro the woods on the Mo. side. He was overtaken by a full-grown man and he shot that boy dead.' This anecdote, repeated in *Life on the Mississippi* the following year, obviously became the source of the ambuscade incident in *Huckleberry Finn* when Bud Grangerford, Buck's cousin, is shot by Baldy Shepherdson.

Despite these additions, however, we now know that Twain wrote the substance of the feud chapters before his visit to the South. It is also likely that he had begun work on the king/duke sequences well before the second, major sitting when the novel was completed in 1883. These facts were uncovered by Walter Blair, who in 1958 published research superseding DeVoto's. Blair's conclusions, summarised in *Mark Twain and Huck Finn* (1960), were based on analyses of Twain's inks, papers and writing habits, together with other evidence drawn from unpublished material. They were that Twain actually returned to work on the novel in October, 1879, substantially completing the Grangerford-Shepherdson episodes in the course of the next eight months, that is, by June, 1880. Blair also concluded that between this period and mid-June, 1883, Twain began work on the next section (introducing the king and the duke, the dramatic account of Boggs's death at Sherburn's hand), before settling down to finish the whole at Quarry Farm, Elmira, later that summer. Finally, as we have already noted, the novel was extensively revised through the winter of 1884.

Blair's researches thus support a critical reading which emphasises the novel's close structural unity and singleness of thought. The first sixteen chapters of *Huckleberry Finn* contain all the elements that are subsequently developed and extended in the rest of the novel. And these seem to have been present from the first, Twain perceiving his direction and understanding his intellectual stress from the earliest formulation.

2

Dialectic of Form and Structure

For a novel that leaves behind such an overwhelming sense of movement, *Huckleberry Finn* is extraordinarily static. The impression of almost continuous motion is of course deliberate, deriving in part from the genuine rush and tug of the river, but also from the multitude of sharply drawn characters, like the oily undertaker at Wilks' funeral, or the massed personality of the circus crowd laughing at the fake drunk. Above all, however, this is a novel of continual flight and escape, a movement that begins in playfulness in the second chapter (Huck slipping from the house) but which hastens into genuine fleeing rapidly thereafter. Huck, and then Huck-and-Jim, and finally Huck alone again, retreat and evade throughout the action until, in the novel's many-sided conclusion, Huck ducks out for the last time.

Much of the tension in the novel derives from the close interplay between its sense of perpetual movement and its actual stasis. The effect is genuinely dialectical in the Marxian sense since the initial motion gives rise to the fixity that in turn creates the conditions for further geographic change. Hamlin Hill, editor of the facsimile first edition, is thus only half-right when he divides the novel structurally into four parts dominated by change: St. Petersburg and Jackson's Island (chapters one to eleven), Jackson's Island to the Grangerfords' (chapters twelve to sixteen), the Grangerfords' to the Phelpses' (chapters seventeen to thirty-one), and the Evasion (chapters thirty-two to forty-three). Hill's stress is all on flow and alteration:

> The most obvious thing about this division is its geographical basis, with its emphasis on motion – movement down the Mississippi. As in any picaresque novel, action and movement are essential to *Huckleberry Finn*; two middle sections of progression down the river are framed by the two static sections at St. Petersburg and Uncle Silas's farm.
>
> (*Adventures of Huckleberry Finn*, California, 1962, p.x.)

17

But though this account has symmetry it overlooks important things. First, the situation at the Phelpses' is precisely not static but spills out into Jim's escape and Huck's last farewell. Secondly, the three families with which Huck becomes involved in his adventures (the Grangerfords, the Wilkses and the Phelpses) approximate sufficiently for a blurring of identity to occur. Thus when Tom Sawyer re-emerges at the novel's end, part of our frustration, as readers, is that Huck seems to have got nowhere in his headlong flight. Twain returns him exactly to square one. This is one of the reasons his final decision to light out once again is such a relief. Hill's analysis, the conventional one, therefore literally mistakes Twain's conscious dialectic, confusing alteration with stasis and fluidity with inertia. What Hill does not see is how each negates the other.

One's recollection of *Huckleberry Finn* then is of many faces. However, if we tease apart the novel's narrative structure we find that it is surprisingly motionless, focussing on a handful of pivotal episodes rather than a concatenation of rapid change. Further, each of these sequences relates closely to the others, both at surface levels and at the level of the book's darker meaning. This is part of what we have characterised as the dialectic of form. A fuller analysis will illustrate this.

Huckleberry Finn rests on quadrant of organisational pillars, four points of contact with the land which are integrated and played off dialectically against the flowing progress of the river. Each point, additionally, registers a stage in Huck's journey, both geographic and moral, since the two are deliberately entangled. This explanation partly accounts for the artistically unsatisfying impact of the novel's closing stages: Tom Sawyer's return to the home of one of his relatives, together with Huck's evasive resistance to civilisation, in fact recreates both the *milieu* and mentality of St Petersburg (Hannibal). The process of alteration is abruptly terminated and we are fed the palliative of Huck's retreat instead. The action becomes circular rather than progressive.

The novel's first section is given to St Petersburg and Pap Finn. Its tone is one of physical constraint and fear: Huck is imprisoned and, at one point, in mortal danger. Pap's knife is against his throat; the cabin is isolated; the door is sealed. Yet already a sense of Huck's developing maturity is established, largely by the contrast between the childish games of bloodletting and escape he

18

plays in chapter two and the serious manoeuvres in his real world when he has to dissemble his own death in order to escape Pap and survive. The flight from his father is the push that gives the novel its impetus.

Simultaneously the deeply psycho-sexual themes of death and rebirth, never far below the surface in this novel, are introduced for the first time. I am not suggesting Twain ever read Freud or his precursors; nevertheless, following Lawrence, we have to trust the tale. It is clear that in the hog-slaying sequence, for example, Twain is either consciously or unconsciously picking up in an Oedipal way his earlier image of Pap as a drunken pig. The point is made even more dramatically when Huck, in an entirely practical way of course, uses the hog's blood and the weight of its body dragged through the undergrowth to suggest his own: a pointer to his affinity with his father which looks ahead in a covert way to his own eventual adulthood. Equally, Huck's forced escape from the small, imprisoning cabin, in blood and undergrowth and through the small hole he cuts at the back, is an image of rebirth and renewal.

Twain's dialectic is never more profound than at this moment since from this point in the novel Huck is officially dead. Thus the nearness of death at Pap's hands leads to Huck's rebirth which in turn is achieved through a literal-symbolic murder. It is the negation of the negation. Twain is careful to underscore his point by allowing Huck, and hence the reader, to witness the gruesome search for his dead body: the cannon to force his corpse to the surface of the water, the mercury-laden loaves to lead the seekers to what Huck calls his 'remainders'. Again the dialectical note is struck: the bread indeed locates the corpse, but only to give it further life. 'I took out the plug and shook out the little dab of quicksilver, and set my teeth in. It was "baker's bread" − what the quality eat − none of your lowdown cornpone.' Twain of course seizes the opportunity to provide a striking image of social differentiation, together with the understated irony that Huck has first to die before St Petersburg will feed him decently.

Twain never quite lets us forget the fact of Huck's official death. When he meets Jim subsequently on the island the runaway is at first terrified, taking him for a ghost; later, towards the novel's end, we are reminded again by Tom's similar reaction on discovering him at the Phelpses': 'I hain't never done you no harm. You know that. So, then, what you want to come back and ha'nt *me* for?' It occurs to neither of them that Huck may just not have died. Again, some time after encountering the reborn Huck, Jim makes an unconsciously funny remark which, in a two-edged way, stresses Twain's point: 'I 'uz powerful sorry you's killed, Huck, but I ain't no mo', now.' The cutting edge is that, even for Jim, Huck has not yet been restored to life. Throughout the rest of the action Huck is reincarnated in a series of aliases: as Sarah Williams, Mary Williams and Sarah Mary Williams; as George Peters; as George Jackson; as Adolphus, the English servant to the king and duke; and finally as Tom Sawyer when he feels that 'it was like being born again, I was so glad to find out who I was.'

In this first section Huck achieves a kind of self-parturition when he takes the first intelligent initiative of his life, the cunning escape from Pap. It is almost simultaneous with his maturing attitude towards Jim. By the time he and the slave decide to fly the island they have become comrades: 'They're after us!' Huck calls out, although they're only after Jim. In other words, Huck's early acts of self-liberation prepare the way for his casting off of the shackles of Southern racist and religious attitudes: Twain's real targets in the novel. Part of his purpose is to show how the two prejudices are connected.

Twain's was a genius peculiarly obsessed with subterranean images of wombs and rebirth and still-born children. Even his adult figures are curiously immature. Further, entombing caverns dominate his best fiction: in *Tom Sawyer*, in *A Connecticut Yankee*, and, of course, in the early chapters of *Huckleberry Finn*. In almost every case children or young people are hidden unnaturally in the earth. Kenneth Lynn has pointed out, in addition, that in his travels in Europe Twain was most powerfully attracted to prisons, dungeons, tombs and catacombs, and wrote about them with exceptional vividness: the solitary confinement cells in the Chateau d'If, for instance, portrayed with such stylistic vigour in *The Innocents Abroad*.

His fiction might have been full of caverns, but in Twain's memory and psyche there was only one: 'our great cave, three miles below Hannibal', described unforgettably in his *Autobiography*. The imagery he uses when speaking of it is unmistakably sexual: it was 'a tangled wilderness of narrow and lofty clefts and passages. . .an easy place to get lost in.' But what turned it into the eternal symbolic womb was the following extraordinary fact which appears to have become deeply embedded in Twain's subconscious, rising repeatedly at critical moments in his creative life:

> The cave was an uncanny place, for it contained a corpse – the corpse of a young girl of fourteen. It was in a glass cylinder inclosed in a copper one which was suspended from a rail which bridged a narrow passage. The body was preserved in alcohol, and it was said that loafers and rowdies used to drag it up by the hair and look at the dead face. The girl was the daughter of a St Louis surgeon of extraordinary ability and wide celebrity. He was an eccentric man and did many strange things. He put the poor thing in that forlorn place himself.
>
> (*Mark Twain's Autobiography*, I, pp. 105-6.)

Twain seems to have understood in an unconscious way the pathetic, life-affirming gesture of the grief-stricken father who re-enacted with such grotesque symbolism the process of fertilisation and gestation. In *Huckleberry Finn* he included an episode which resonates on the same level, situating it just after Huck's flight from his father and before his adoption by the Grangerfords as 'George Jackson.' Perhaps even more significantly, it was precisely this episode, known as the 'raftsman's passage', that Twain decided to excise from the novel in 1883. He replaced it, as we have noted, with the adventure on board the grounded *Walter Scott,* a sequence which resembles it in some important respects but in which the emphasis has shifted from images of confinement, infanticide and rebirth to the more overtly political and moral. The change appears to reflect the switched emphasis in the novel itself: from a boyhood fantasy to a statement with strong social implications.

The excised chapter goes as follows. Having been lost in the fog, Huck tries to find out where he and Jim are by hiding aboard a large raft and trying to overhear the speakers. In the dark – an important image as we shall see – Huck slips on board and listens to the blarney and songs of the raftsmen. One story tells of a man called Dick Allbright who was pursued on the river by a dreadful barrel that floated after him wherever he went. Its presence brought destruction and fear; it could never be shaken off.

Finally, in desperation, the barrel is hauled aboard Dick Albright's raft. It is forced open. Inside they find – the corpse of a baby.

It is of course Dick Allbright's child, Charles William Allbright, choked to death one night by his enraged father and hidden in the barrel. For three years it has pursued him.

Suddenly Huck is discovered by the raftsmen. They surround him, demand to know his name, and Huck replies: 'Charles William Allbright'. Of course it is a joke, both by Huck and Mark Twain, but its reverberations extend far beyond itself, echoing back to the trapped Huck in his father's cabin, his escape, his sequence of rebirths and to the little girl in Hannibal's cave; to the curious circumstances of Pap's death, whose naked body floats down the river after Huck in a wooden house bestrewn with women's underwear and obscene drawings; and finally to the fantastic ceremony of Jim's elaborate escape through a tunnel dug at the rear of his own wooden prison.

 The novel's second section, the Grangerford sequence, is also dominated by images of grief and death. But where the feud is the focus here the tone is given by the grotesque spirit of Emmeline Grangerford, whose morbidity is preserved so reverently by her family. References to mourning and blackness are thick in these pages: Emmeline's drawings are 'blacker, mostly, than is common', with bereaved figures wearing 'black slippers,' ankles crossed about with 'black tape', and carrying in their hands letters fixed with 'black sealing wax'. The white-washed walls of the house serve only to emphasise the contrast.

It is too easy to dismiss Emmeline with a laugh. Like the surgeon's daughter she is preserved in emotional formaldehyde:

> They kept Emmeline's room trim and nice and all the things fixed in it just the way the she liked to have them when she was alive, and nobody ever slept there. The old lady took care of the room herself, though there was plenty of niggers, and she sewed there a good deal and read her bible there, mostly.

Emmeline's last, uncompleted picture, the girl with the six arms, is kept 'over the head of her bed in her room, and every time her birthday come they hung flowers on it. Other times it was hid with a little curtain'. (*Huckleberry Finn, Chapter 17.*)

Twain reveals his psychological acuity here. Critics who take these passages as jest, or who compare Emmeline's dreadful, sentimental verse to the mawkish poetry of real-life Victorian American ladies, like Julia A. Moore, whose *Sentimental Song Book* was owned by Twain, wholly miss the point. Emmeline ritualises and orders the experience of death for her family. Through the elaborate weepings in her drawings and verse, together with her tough, business-like insistence on the universality of dying, she prepares the Grangerfords for their inevitable catastrophe. She 'kept a scrapbook when she was alive, and used to paste obituaries and accidents and cases of patient suffering in it out of the *Presbyterian Observer*, and write poetry after them out of her own head.' Death could have no dominion in the presence of Emmeline Grangerford:

> Every time a man died, or a woman died, or a child died, she would be on hand with her 'tribute' before he was cold. She called them tributes. The neighbours said it was the doctor first, then Emmeline, then the undertaker – the undertaker never got in ahead of Emmeline but once, and then she hung fire on a rhyme for the dead person's name, which was Whistler.

(Huckleberry Finn, Chapter 17.)

But for Huck and the reader Emmeline's morbidness serves only to intensify the horror of death. The ghastly 'Ode to Stephen Dowling Bots, Dec'd.', the boy 'that fell down a well and was drownded', looks ahead in its mourning to the death of Buck Grangerford, murdered by the Shepherdsons. Huck's quiet description not only contrasts with Emmeline's; it is made possible, and rendered intense, precisely because of what has gone before:

> When I got down out of the tree, I crept along down the river bank a piece, and found the two bodies laying in the edge of the water, and tugged at them till I got them ashore; then I covered up their faces, and got away as quick as I could. I cried a little when I was covering up Buck's face, for he was mighty good to me.

(Huckleberry Finn, Chapter 18.)

Again we may note the characteristically dialectical narrative strategy Twain employs in this novel: farce ripens into tragedy,

ation, and then moves the action on. As we shall see, this
repeats itself so persistently throughout that it becomes
...'s defining mode.

In this section of the novel Huck is largely inactive. He is a
helpless spectator and of course judge; and his verdict is severe.
Nevertheless he intervenes only to the extent of acting as go-
between for Harney Shepherdson and Sophia Grangerford, thus
unwittingly precipitating the final slaughter. It is significant that
Huck's single act is for love and reconciliation, and this is one of
the reasons he does not hold himself too heavily responsible for
the tragedy. He does reflect that he might have gone to Colonel
Grangerford in the first instance, but by this stage he has
learned already to reject social duty when it conflicts with his
inner promptings. There is no question of Hegelian, and therefore potentially tragic, antagonisms here. He is Sophia's Friar
Lawrence. Huck understands, with his growing maturity, that the
violence and death were endemic. He escapes again with relief to
his next incarnation.

What Huck leaves behind, of course, is not merely George
Jackson and the dead Grangerfords. The religion of loving thy
neighbour and turning the other cheek is the real fatality of the
feud. In this section Twain quite deliberately exposes Christianity as morbid and hypocritical, its adherents hating where
they should love, and killing where they should give life. In 1885,
the year in which *Huckleberry Finn* was published in America,
Twain wrote to Howells attacking Christianity as 'a loathesome
thing', (*The Portable Mark Twain*, p. 761) and the sentiment
is reflected in his fiction. The Catholic Church is Hank Morgan's
greatest opponent in *A Connecticut Yankee*; in *Huckleberry Finn*
it is the butt of Twain's most vicious sallies. One of the ironies
of the Romeo-and-Juliet theme in this section is that the lovers
do not suceed in reuniting their families. The very opposite
results. The feud chapters thus give further point and emphasis
to the two dimensions of the novel we have already characterised
as Twain's major themes: the corruptness of religion and the
falsity of public attitudes. It is Huck's actions and judgments, in
rejecting both, that make these positions graphic and concrete.

The novel's third section is introduced by the coming of the
phoney king and duke, the figures who most exemplify and represent the alienating power of the cash nexus in nineteenth

24

century America. Yet even in this section death is the dominating presence since the action pivots on the fact of Peter Wilks's funeral. It is a funeral and death without the morbidity of Emmeline Grangerford, however, because Twain's emphasis has shifted away from the fact of social violence to wider problems of social organisation. Inheritance and property rights are the focus here, and especially of course (as we will later discuss in more detail) the non-existent power of Wilks's slaves to decide their own fate.

The king and the duke are out to cheat the dead man's family of his property, and they very nearly succeed. Their weapons are their own cynicism and effrontery, and the gullibility of the family and village who, incredibly, accept their story that they are Wilks's long-lost English relatives come to claim their inheritance. Twain is driven to stretch coincidence desperately here, coming close to violating one of his own literary precepts – that 'the personages of a tale shall confine themselves to possibilities and let miracles alone; or, if they venture a miracle, the author must so plausibly set it forth as to make it look possible and reasonable.' ('Fenimore Cooper's Literary Offenses', *The Portable Mark Twain*, p. 543). Twain just squeezes by on this one, but only until he arranges for the real relatives to turn up – unable to identify themselves because of mislaid baggage, and unable to provide a specimen of handwriting because of a recently broken arm. Twain rapidly winds the story up after this with the rediscovery of the gold, the exposure of the imposters, and Huck's renewed flight after identity.

Concealment and of course deception are the themes here: expressed primarily in the serious play-acting of the king and the duke (anticipated by the farcical renderings of Shakespeare earlier) and Huck's hiding of the treasure in Wilks's coffin, but also in Huck's assumption of a new alias and role as servant to the imposters, and his gulling of the king and duke themselves in conclusion. Huck deceives the master dissemblers who are thus out-dissembled.

At all levels in these chapters Huck achieves his greatest independence and maturity. He intervenes decisively in affecting the outcome of the charade, and at the same time reaches the two insights which, together with the lessons learned at the Grangerfords', are the source of most of the novel's positive values. These

25

are, first, his celebrated decision not to betray Jim, and thus to go to Hell; and secondly, his moment of cynical pity when he watches the king and the duke being tarred and feathered.

Too much of the wrong kind of emphasis, in my opinion, has been placed on Huck's resolution to face everlasting fire rather than betray his friend. By this juncture in the novel Christianity has been lengthily discussed and rejected, not only by Twain and the reader but by Huck as well. Hell carries few terrors for the boy who, on the novel's third page, has already declared his wish to go 'to the bad place'. Heaven is the domain of the oppressive Miss Watson and, 'Well, I couldn't see no advantage in going where she was going, so I made up my mind I wouldn't try for it. . . .I asked her if she reckoned Tom Sawyer would go there, and she said, not by a considerable sight. I was glad about that, because I wanted him and me to be together.' (*Huckleberry Finn*, Chapter 1.)

On the novel's structural level these two passages – Huck's early rejection of Heaven, his later decision to accept damnation – are further instances of Twain's dialectical counterposing of the frivolous and the profound. Within the overall framework of values, however, Huck's resolve not to betray Jim acts on a societal rather than a metaphysical plane. It constitutes his final condemnation of slavery and all its works. At the same time, and in so doing, Huck sets himself against both the form of social organisation which has institutionalised the system and its self-justifying, hypocritical ideology. By this point in the action the notion of wickedness, which Huck here consciously espouses, has become associated with all that is human, decent and honest. Huck's resolution thus exposes the depth of Christian double-think where love is hate, honesty is deception, freedom is bondage, loyalty is treason and friendship is enmity.

Huck considers writing to Miss Watson to tell her that Jim is imprisoned at the Phelpses'. He writes; he lays the note on the ground.

It was a close place. I took it up, and held it in my hand. I was a-trembling, because I'd got to decide, forever, betwixt two things, and I knowed it. I studied a minute, sort of holding my breath, and then says to myself:
'All right, then, I'll *go* to hell' – and tore it up.

26

It was awful thoughts, and awful words, but they
And I let them stay said; and never thought no more
forming. I shoved the whole thing out of my head; a
would take up wickedness again, which was in my lin
brung up to it, and the other warn't. And for a starter,
go to work and steal Jim out of slavery again; and if I could
think up anything worse, I would do that, too; because as long
as I was in, and in for good, I might as well go the whole hog.
                                    (*Huckleberry Finn*, Chapter 31.)

Huck's decision is vindicated a few pages later when he and
Tom Sawyer watch the God-fearing Christians of the area railroad
the king and the duke out of town, tarred and feathered. Huck's
compassion is more genuinely Christian than any emotion the
mob might feel, for he has a real grievance against the two men. It
was they, after all, who sold Jim back into slavery for the Judas-
like sum, as Tony Tanner puts it, of 'forty dirty dollars'. Yet the
fourteen year-old Huck is capable of an unexpectedly mature
response, pity rather than satisfaction, and backs it up with a
generalising insight into the nature of humanity beyond his
years. Huck's reaction marks the distance he has travelled from
the days of his membership of Tom Sawyer's Gang, and Tom's
presence serves to emphasise the fact. Again the scene is set in
darkness, the night lit only by the flaming torches of the
screaming, brutalised crowd. Twain depicts them as barbarians:

. . .and as we struck into the town and up through the middle
of it — it was as much as half-after eight, then — here comes a
raging rush of people, with torches, and an awful whooping and
yelling, and banging tin pans and blowing horns; and we jumped
to one side to let them go by; and as they went by, I see they
had the king and the duke astraddle of a rail — that is, I knowed
it *was* the king and the duke, though they was all over tar and
feathers, and didn't look like nothing in the world that was
human — just looked like a couple of monstrous big soldier-
plumes. Well, it made me sick to see it; and I was sorry for them
poor pitiful rascals, it seemed like I couldn't ever feel any hard-
ness against them any more in the world. It was a dreadful thing
to see. Human beings *can* be awful cruel to one another.
                                    (*Huckleberry Finn*, Chapter 33.)

After witnessing this Huck 'pokes' along back home, feeling 'kind of ornery, and humble, and to blame, somehow.' His depression and nausea deliberately recall his emotions when watching the massacre of the Grangerford boys. The two episodes are comparable in the sadism and blood-lust of the mobs, but in the earlier Huck is not yet ready to draw the moral inference. This is part of Twain's point:

> All of sudden, bang! bang! bang! goes three or four guns — the men had slipped around through the woods and come in from behind without their horses! The boys jumped for the river — both of them hurt — and as they swum down the current the men run along the bank shooting at them and singing out, 'Kill them, kill them!' It made me so sick I most fell out of the tree. I ain't agoing to tell *all* that happened — it would make me sick again if I was to do that. I wished I hadn't ever come ashore that night, to see such things. I ain't ever going to get shut of them — lots of times I dream about them.

> (*Huckleberry Finn*, Chapter 18.)

It may be significant that on this occasion Huck does not even consider the possibility of action, of involvement. Of course he is helpless, and can only look on until the killing is over. Then he performs his primitive little burial rite over Buck: covering the dead face, weeping in tribute. In the later episode, however, with the king and the duke, though he and Tom are equally powerless, Huck does think of intervening. Unhappily 'we see we was too late — couldn't do no good.' Part of Huck's lesson is the indissolubility of action and conviction.

The pattern of the novel to this point has been the developing interplay between Huck's maturing values and his capacity for direct intervention in the world. The process is not exactly dialectical, although each succeeding episode leads into a fresh perception which creates the conditions for the next episode. In the St Petersburg chapters Huck was wholly passive, submitting to his father's will, accepting the constraints of the Widow Douglas and Miss Watson, allowing himself to be controlled and, finally, imprisoned. Yet it was precisely this early sense of moral and physical claustrophobia that led to his initial successful bid for space and freedom. His flight, in its headlong impetus,

28

involved him increasingly with others and with the need to act in their world. This is the paradox and tension in Huck's career. The more he struggles to be free, the less free he is. 'I wished I hadn't come ashore that night, to see such things.' The alliance with Jim was at first fundamentally passive, a simple mitigation of his loneliness. Even his early decision not to betray the runaway represented inaction rather than commitment, a conscious decision *not* to act. As the plot develops, however, this resolution transforms itself by stages into the positive act of breaking Jim out of his prison. One of the milestones in Huck's progress along this road is when he lies to the white slave-hunters about the small-pox on his raft. At the same time, in a parallel transformation, his maturing convictions are marked by the two episodes which increasingly demand his active involvement: the Granderford-Shepherdson sequence and the situation at the Wilks funeral. The shift is clearly to the active.

The last fifth of the novel, then, is exactly where we would expect to find the vital integration of everything Huck has become: an intellectually freer individual with a marked capacity for independent action. Jim's situation demands it, Huck's abilities are up to it, and his resolution requires it: 'I would go to work and steal Jim out of slavery again.' Instead, at the Phelpses' farm, which is where the novel's final section is situated, he fades as a moral and active being. Tom Sawyer returns, Huckleberry Finn evaporates. This is the reason so many readers have found the novel's conclusion profoundly bathetic.

Twain not only frustrates our aroused expectations but he does so in a particularly irritating way. Tom Sawyer's return is an insult to the reader, for he is restored to the action by way of the crudest narrative manipulations, a set of coincidences so farfetched as to render almost credible the absurd congruence of people and events at Wilks's funeral. First and foremost, Jim 'just happens' to have been sold back into bondage to one of Tom Sawyer's relatives. This outrageous contrivance − Jim has supposedly travelled 1,100 miles from St Petersburg, the king and the duke to have despatched him at random − is the structural lynchpin of everything that follows. The whole thing creaks dangerously about this point. Secondly, the Phelpses 'just happen' at that time to be coincidentally expecting Tom − but, luckily as it turns out, not his brother Sid − on a rare and pointless visit.

Another loosely-fitted narrative bolt. Thirdly, Aunt Sally 'just happens' to mistake Huck for Tom, conveniently (a) not having met Tom before, (b) overlooking Huck's shabby clothes and (c) giving him his cue — 'It's *Tom Sawyer*!' — before he can say anything and spoil his opportunity. A little while later Tom 'just happens' to turn up in time to pose credibly as Sid. The fact that Huck Finn 'just happens' to know intimately the person he is mistaken for — in fact, Tom is virtually the only other person in the world Huck knows so intimately — thus luckily provides him with the perfect cover. And so on. Twain's narrative arrangements here are hardly worthy of him or his great novel.

Huckleberry Finn all but collapses at this point. It does so because Twain, as in the Wilks episode, forgets his own literary principles.

In 'Fenimore Cooper's Literary Offenses' Twain defines the art of fiction, as he understood it, by listing with merciless wit eighteen crimes against the Muse committed by the author of *The Deerslayer*. The thrust of his case, illustrated by humorous examples from the Leatherstocking series, is that a novel must be credible, or at least plausible, and that an author should not subvert the possible by resorting to the absurd. One of Twain's striking examples is the way Cooper allows three riflemen to pump their bullets, one after the other, into the same bullet hole one hundred yards away. In short, 'Fenimore Cooper's Literary Offenses' is one of the important documents of nineteenth century literary realism. The rules of fiction, Twain declares, require among other things

> that the episodes of a tale shall be necessary parts of the tale and shall help to develop it. . .that the personages in a tale, both dead and alive, shall exhibit sufficient cause for being there. . .that crass stupidities shall not be played upon the reader. . .

> (*The Portable Mark Twain*, pp. 542-3.)

But these precepts are grossly violated by the author of the evasion chapters in *Huckleberry Finn*. Tom's sudden return is wholly unnecessary, and does nothing to develop the action; quite insufficient cause is offered to account for his suddenly being where he is; and the risible coincidences which establish the conditions for the novel's concluding chapters can only be

30

described as crass stupidities played upon the reader. The convergence of Tom, Huck and Jim in the same wooden hut at the Phelpses' is as ridiculous, in its own manner, as Hawkeye's ability to shoot a bullet perfectly into a hole the size of a nail head three hundred feet away.

Unhappily, the absurdities are not ended with Jim's fortuitous purchase or Tom's unexpected return to the action. Twain appears to have felt compelled for obscure reasons to introduce further incredible manipulations and puerile slapstick to help his plot along. The main situation, Jim's captivity, is meant to suit the exigencies of Tom's romantic spirit and, although it is hardly credible at this point in the novel, both Huck and Jim willingly allow themselves to be domineered by him. This, in spite of the carefully dramatised moral and personal growth they have both sustained. Consequently they are diminished as characters. Jim forfeits his dignity, his manhood, his three-dimensionality, reverting once again to stage-niggerdom; Huckleberry Finn loses his identity altogether. He becomes Jo Harper, Ben Rogers – any of Tom's sidekicks.

The lowest point in this sequence is the childish humour in which Twain inexplicably indulges. And yet, though unclear, his motives seem bound up in a curious way with his own early life. One of his unfunniest jokes, for instance, recalls at every point a richly amusing passage from the *Autobiography* describing a childhood incident. Again the cave at Hannibal is a dominating presence:

Along outside of the front fence ran the country road, dusty in the summertime, and a good place for snakes – they liked to lie in it and sun themselves; when they were rattlesnakes or puff adders, we killed them; when they were black snakes, or racers, or belonged to the fabled 'hoop' breed, we fled, without shame; when they were 'house snakes,' or 'garters,' we carried them home and put them in Aunt Patsy's work basket for a surprise; for she was prejudiced against snakes, and always when she took the basket in her lap and they began to climb out of it it disordered her mind. She never could seem to get used to them; her opportunities went for nothing. And she was always cold toward bats, too, and could not bear them; and yet I think a bat is as friendly a bird as

31

there is. My mother was Aunt Patsy's sister and had the same wild superstitions. A bat is beautifully soft and silky; I do not know any creature that is pleasanter to the touch or more grateful for caressings, if offered in the right spirit. I know all about these coleoptera, because our great cave, three miles below Hannibal, was multitudinously stocked with them, and often I brought them home to amuse my mother with. It was easy to manage if it was a school day, because then I had ostensibly been to school and hadn't any bats. She was not a suspicious person, but full of trust and confidence; and when I said, 'There's something in my coat pocket for you,' she would put her hand in. But she always took it out again, herself; I didn't have to tell her. It was remarkable, the way she couldn't learn to like private bats. The more experience she had, the more she could not change her views.

(*Mark Twain's Autobiography*, pp. 103-4.)

Twain is in his element here as the complete and almost archetypal Southern humorist: deadpan, gentle, eyes twinkling. The more outrageous he becomes the more expressionless grows his voice. The strength of this passage derives precisely from its imprecision, its broad comedy from its understatement. Aunt Patsy's reaction in finding a snake crawling from her sewing basket is hilarious because Twain doesn't spell it out; he merely says, in his innocent way, that it 'disordered' her mind. Equally, his mother simply takes her hand out of his pocket again: the joke lies in the fact that Twain avoids slapstick just when you're expecting it. Binding it all together is Twain's evident personal charm and the love he bears both for himself when young and for his mother.

In *Huckleberry Finn*, however, the gentleness and charm are gone, and the understatement has become the crudest over-stress. All the jokes are in red ink. The kindly humour has become mere brashness and where you would expect to find slapstick you get it — multiplied. The result is that the joke palls immediately, becomes tiresome as it continues and then embarrassing as Twain plays it out to the very end. The situation is that Tom and Huck have collected together 'a couple of dozen garters and house-snakes' for Jim's crypt, but during supper they manage to escape:

But it didn't matter much, because they was still on the pre-
mises somewheres. So we judged we could get some of them
again. No, there warn't no real scarcity of snakes about the
house for a considerble spell. You'd see them dripping from
the rafters and places, every now and then; and they generly
landed in your plate, or down the back of your neck, and most
of the time where you didn't want them. Well, they was hand-
some, and striped, and there warn't no harm in a million of
them; but that never made no difference to Aunt Sally, she
despised snakes, be the breed what they might, and she
couldn't stand them no way you could fix it; and every time
one of them flopped down on her, it didn't make no difference what she was doing, she would just lay that work
down and light out. I never see such a woman. And you could
hear her whoop to Jericho. You couldn't get her to take aholt
of one of one of them with the tongs. And if she turned over
and found one in bed, she would scramble out and lift a howl
that you would think the house was afire. She disturbed the
old man so, that he said he could most wish there hadn't ever
been no snakes created. Why, after every last snake had been
gone clear out of the house for as much as a week, Aunt Sally
warn't over it yet; she warn't near over it; when she was setting thinking about something, you could touch her on the
back of her neck with a feather and she would jump right out
of her stockings. It was very curious. But Tom said all women
was just so. He said they was made that way; for some reason
or other.

(Huckleberry Finn, Chapter 39.)

Twain is clearly reaching for the same effect here, but misses
it substantially. He betrays his artistic insecurity by making Huck
overwrite, use words which for him are out of character in their
metaphorical richness. The snakes 'dripped' from the rafters,
'flopped' onto Aunt Sally; and, finally, we are left unconvinced.
Just how many snakes could two boys collect in one basket?

These pale jests. and the unbelievable coincidences which are
both their basis and the necessary conditions for all that happens
in these chapters, are offered by Twain to justify and account for
the elaborate birth-ritual surrounding Jim's release. For Jim
merely to walk out of the cabin door, we are led to believe, is too

simple for Tom Sawyer. More, we are asked to accept that a recaptured runaway slave, facing bondage and punishment, would sit for days and nights on end in an open prison playing at an obscure game whose meaning is known only to an adolescent boy. He is supposed to do this while a long tunnel is dug at the back of his shed so that he can crawl out that way to freedom.

Further silly contrivances are introduced to account for Tom's irresponsibility here. Miss Watson, perfectly healthy when we saw her last, has 'just happened' to die a few weeks previously. Luckily for Jim she remembered him in her dying moments and, overcome by an unexplained emotion, whispered a deathbed manumission. Luckily Tom has heard about it, luckily he is believed when he finally reveals all, luckily no one is killed in the evasion attempt.

The novel's closing sequences thus become an unfunny charade in which Tom (and Twain) mock Huck, Jim and the reader, leading us all through a series of irrelevant hoops. Or almost irrelevant, as we shall see. There remains the remote possibility that Twain intended a connection between Miss Watson's death and Jim's rebirth, a clumsy symbolic enactment of parturition, but I am unpersuaded of this. What is more pertinent is that Tom's contrived adolescent ceremony nearly botches the whole escape. Indeed, the whole evasion *is* botched, and Jim comes within a heart-beat of re-enslavement. The Phelpses and their friends, alerted by Tom's blood-curdling warnings, arrive at the shed armed and in a murderous mood. We have met this mob previously in the novel: confronting Sherburn, massacring the Grangerford boys, tarring and feathering the king and the duke. Jim, Huck and Tom just manage to evade them, though not without cost: Tom is severely wounded by a shot. The consequences of this, both actual and potential, are disastrous. His death would of course be a tragedy for himself and his family; but it would be almost equally serious for Jim. Tom is after all the only person who can identify him as a free man. Even in the event, although Jim is ultimately released because of Tom's intervention, he is at first recaptured, beaten, and reimprisoned.

Still, although these chapters fail as art, their meaning and significance within the novel's moral framework seem quite clear. Tom is manifestly at fault; he has played loosely with his own life and another man's freedom. He is the victim of some viral strain of Sir Walterism. Twain points the fact by allowing him to pay Jim off with money, the same sum — forty dollars — for which he was betrayed by the treacherous king and duke. The boy's mind is so corrupted by cheap romantic fiction — and indeed by some of the world's finest writing too — that he has irresponsibly lost all contact with reality. The actual world with its well-oiled carbines brings down not only his fairy castle but, literally, the fantasist himself. The single redeeming feature of these disappointing final chapters is Twain's muted but nevertheless resolute assault upon Tom Sawyerism.

Adventures of Huckleberry Finn thus comes as close as any novel might dare to total failure. And yet Twain snatches artistic victory at the very edge of this yawning defeat, though the reverse was so nearly true. It is, however, a false and unrepeatable triumph, since he achieves it through poetry and verbal sleight-of-hand rather than through the genuine redemption of his central figure in action. Huck finally does not come into his own; instead Twain offers us a shallow technical equilibrium wrapped together with a dazzling display of linguistic brilliance.

We noted earlier that what the novel called for at the outset of the evasion chapters was a striking gesture of independence from Huck, basing his action on a strongly felt and argued moral case. Instead we were fed Tom Sawyer's dreams. Ultimately, however, Huck is permitted an active gesture, though what he does represents a serious avoidance of all the real issues previously raised. The novel's last two sentences, probably the most frequently quoted valedictory in the history of fiction, actually cheat Twain through to an acceptable conclusion because of the sheer verbal glitter he employs. They are literally unforgettable:

> But I reckon I got to light out for the Territory ahead of the rest, because Aunt Sally she's going to adopt me and sivilize me, and I can't stand it. I been there before.
>
> (*Huckleberry Finn*, Chapter 43.)

The overwhelming charm of it, of that innocently mis-spelt word, of the bad grammar, of the mischievous cynical defiance Huck displays in his final sentence, has blinded with its coruscation repeated generations of critics. But in fact it's a confession of failure. Huck is exactly where he was on page one: 'The Widow Douglas, she took me for her son, and allowed she would

35

sivileze me; but. . .when I couldn't stand it no longer, I lit out.' Huck, for all his moral and personal evolution between these points, is finally – Peter Pan, and off he wings to Never-Never Land. The nearest thing to this kind of conclusion in another major work of fiction is Thomas Mann's *The Magic Mountain*, when Hans Castorp disappears into the mud and gunsmoke of Flanders. Mann has justified this finale, however, within the historical, philosophical *and* artistic perspectives of his novel, since by its end Hans and the War have become consciously emblematic of the old dying European order and the *coup de grace* which is to dispose of it. Yet even here Mann avoids Twain's finality, fixing ultimately and with greater honesty than the earlier writer upon a stark, concluding question mark. But Huck is gone forever, and though Twain returned him nominally to the foreground in later works – on one occasion even as an aged and dying man – these are only different characters wearing his disguise. Twain was ultimately unable to handle the great and in some ways archetypal figure he had created. And not knowing what to do with him – unable to give him further life, unwilling of course to give him death – he behaved as Merlin with The Boss in *A Connecticut Yankee*. He put him away for eternity.

*   *   *

Marx begins *The Eighteenth Brumaire of Louis Bonaparte* with the remark that all the great facts and personages of history recur, as it were, twice: first as tragedy, then as farce. Marx means this more than humorously; though hardly a historical law, it expresses the operation of the dialectical process even in unanticipated ways. He offers as examples Danton and Caussidiere, Robespierre and Louis Blanc and, of course, the great Napoleon and Napoleon III.

In *Huckleberry Finn* the same dialectic unexpectedly occurs – unexpected because Twain's is not a name commonly associated with Marx's – though occasionally the farcical is allowed to precede the tragic. Thus, for instance, Buck Grangerford's death, as we have noted, is anticipated by the tragical history of Stephen Dowling Bots, Dec'd., and the serious play-acting of the king and the duke is preceded by the slapstick account of their preparations to stage famous scenes from Shakespeare. More consistently, however, Twain's practice recalls Marx's sharp formulation.

Twain employs this device at all levels in his story, both major and minor. In each case the effect is to convey a strong sense of unity and form. Thus on what I've called the minor structural level, the king and the duke mock the Harney Shepherdson-Sophia Grangerford recreation of *Romeo and Juliet* with their own farcical rehearsal of the balcony scene. Equally, the duke's role of deaf-mute at the Wilkses' follows Jim's moving account of his own daughter's deafness.

We have already noted the way in which Huck's pig-hunting refers back to Pap's swinish condition, and how Tom pays Jim off with the same sum he brought to the king and the duke. Other striking echoes and parallels are Pap's drunken death and the mock danger of the fake inebriate clown; Jim falsely bound by the king and duke and then later in seriousness sold back into slavery by them; the mob who seek to lynch Sherburn and the mob who tar and feather the king and the duke; Jim's discussion of the unwisdom of Solomon and the struggle between Pap and Miss Watson for Huck; and the circumstances in which the Shepherdsons shoot Buck to death and those in which the Phelpses wound Tom Sawyer.

On the major structural level there is one outstanding instance: Huck imprisoned in his father's cabin in the early chapters and Jim sequestered with the Phelpses at the end. As we have seen, the affinities between these situations are striking. Both Huck and Jim are incarcerated because they represent a potential pecuniary profit; both are constrained in wooden shacks; and both escape in ways which recall powerful images of birth and evacuation. Twain's intention is obviously to relate the two sets of events in a profound way.

I have said that the function of these echoes is to leave the reader with an overwhelming sense of continuity and rigorous structure. At the same time they are associated with the persistent thematic images of darkness and obscured vision to which I referred earlier. Their function, in turn, is to emphasise the serious and even somber intellectual preoccupations which dominate the action. Thus the gloom which pervades the novel arises from two sources (and then, dialectically, feeds back into them): the repeated midnights in which the story is largely told, and the grim significance of its facts.

Clearly, both kinds of darkness are to be related. For instance, most of the novel's nights are impenetrably and inexplicably black. They are often starless and moonless (the fact is repeatedly commented upon) and, since *Huckleberry Finn* is overwhelmingly a nocturnal adventure, much of the action occurs in a mysterious gloom. Almost all of the evasion chapters, about a fifth of the novel, are set at night; the important closing scenes at Wilks's funeral, when all is revealed, take place in the dark before dawn; Jim and Huck spend most of their time on the raft at night (they hide during the day); and most of the second chapter occurs after midnight. Even the Grangerford sequence, the most daylit of all the novel's episodes, is dominated by the gloom of Emmeline's art (the blackness of her drawings we noted earlier), and Buck is driven to make an oddly unfunny joke when he first encounters Huck. Where was Moses when the lights went out? he demands. Answer: 'Why, he was in the *dark*! That's where he was!' Twain's emphasis is clear. Buck's childish joke actually looks back to the very first chapter where Huck is imaged as the infant Moses 'among the Bulrushers'. It is another striking illustration of Twain's close blue-printing in the novel. Where is Huck when the Grangerford lights go out forever?

Huck's world is thus unnaturally but literally (and symbolically) benighted. Jim's first escape, from St Petersburg, is carried out in conditions so pitchy he is able to board and leave unseen a lighted raft; later, when he and Huck explore the *Walter Scott* (run aground in the night), they have to feel their way slowly with their feet, 'spreading our hands out to fend off the guys, for it was so dark we couldn't see no sign of them'. Then, when their own raft is smashed by the riverboat which overlooks them despite the lantern Huck posts, its remains are lost because of the exceptionally heavy gloom. As Jim says: 'If de night hadn't ben so dark. . .we'd a seed de raf'.' Even when Huck is not in physical danger, while he is being mischievous for example, the darkness in his world is so intense that people looking for each other can pass within inches but see nothing. In a deep sense, as I will argue, Huck stumbles when he sees; not tragically, like Gloucester or Oedipus, for the novel remains a comedy, but still consistently within a troubled framework. In *Following the Equator* Twain observed: 'Everything human is pathetic. The secret source of Humor is not joy but sorrow. There is no humor in heaven.'

Associated with the gloom are the novel's dense and frequent fogs. Their sudden descent imposes a terrifying sightlessness which separates the living, choking the senses, bewildering the mind, releasing destruction and failure into an already precarious universe. Cairo, the pair's original objective and gateway to Jim's liberty, is missed because of it; at another point, in a scene which recalls Ishmael's loss of orientation at the tiller of the *Pequod*, Huck loses his bearings entirely in the fog. It is literally like a death, a journey into eternity with Hell itself as a likely destiny: 'I shot out into the solid white fog, and hadn't no more idea which way I was going than a dead man.' Later Huck emphasises both the surrealism of the experience and its capacity to pervert what is natural:

> I throwed the paddle down. I heard the whoop again; it was behind me yet, but in a different place; it kept coming, and kept changing its place, and I kept answering, till by-and-by it was in front of me again and I knowed the current had swung the canoe's head down stream and I was all right, if that was Jim and not some other raftsman hollering. I couldn't tell nothing about voices in a fog, for nothing don't look natural nor sound natural in a fog.
>
> *(Huckleberry Finn*, Chapter 15.)

This scene links up profoundly with the themes of death and rebirth in the book, for Jim has taken Huck in fact for dead. He welcomes him ecstatically back to life: 'Goodness gracious, is dat you, Huck? En you ain' dead – you ain' drownded – you's back agin? It's too good for true, honey, it's too good for true. Lemme look at you, chile, lemme feel o' you. No, you ain' dead! you's back again, 'live en soun', jis de same ole Huck – de same ole Huck, thanks to goodness!'

It is a pivotal moment, not only within the thematic cycle we have been tracing, but in Huck's intensifying relationship with Jim. At first he mocks the slave's mourning; but afterwards he is overcome with remorse and

> It was fifteen minutes before I could work myself up to go and humble myself to a nigger – but I done it, and I warn't ever sorry for it afterwards, neither. I didn't do him no more mean tricks, and I wouldn't done that one if I'd a

knowed it would make him feel that way.

(Huckleberry Finn, Chapter 15.)

⚫ Huck is reborn with a greater maturity and with a further sloughing off of his racist skin. He is thus bound even more tightly to Jim in an awareness of their common humanity. Death, fog and darkness have paradoxically brought them closer together.

The kind of emphasis I have adopted, underscoring the novel's serious preoccupations and calling attention to its persistent gloom, must not be allowed to obscure Twain's general playfulness. But, on the other hand, the humour in *Huckleberry Finn* has often been exaggerated; as we have seen, many of the supposed jokes are either rather unfunny – like the silly burlesque at the Phelpses' – or are deliberately subverted, as humour, by a grim intent – like the story of Emmeline Grangerford. Of course there are parts of the book which are just funny. Still, *Huckleberry Finn* has had more than justice as a humorous novel.

This has happened for two main reasons. First, there is Twain's general reputation as a clown – a reputation which arose early in his career and one which has never wholly dissipated. Moreover – this is the second reason – Twain was careful to encourage the illusion. At the entrance to *Huckleberry Finn* he sets a caveat calculated to arouse expectations of laughter and comedy:

NOTICE

Persons attempting to find a motive in this narrative will be prosecuted; persons attempting to find a moral in it will be banished; persons attempting to find a plot in it will be shot.

By Order of the Author

per

G.G., Chief of Ordnance

It's a kind of Dantesque injunction in reverse. As we have already seen, however, one doesn't have to look too hard to find plot, moral and motive in abundance. Twain's warning, therefore, need not be taken quite as seriously as some have done. It falls into the category of narrative strategy; by his bluff tone he hopes to disarm criticism. And he had every reason to anticipate it, as the reaction of his narrow-minded contemporaries in and around Boston amply demonstrated. Finally, we may note that towards

40

the end of his career Twain acknowledged that the peculiar durability of his writing, as opposed to that of other Southern humoursits, such as Petroleum V. Naseby and Artemus Ward, lay precisely in the seriousness of his jests. He was also given to remarking that the essence of humour was sorrow. And in fact *Huckleberry Finn*, in my experience, tends to make its readers laugh out loud less often than its contemporary, Henry James's *The Bostonians* (1886), though the comedy is broader. Twain's warning looks in one direction but points us in another; like his novel, the lightheartedness belies itself.

The darkness and gloom which permeates the action, we have said, indicates Twain's tight-lipped purpose. On one level its function is symbolically almost conventional: the Mississippi valley in the 1840s was a black spot on the earth. For Twain, as we will see in greater detail presently, the darkness was slavery, a socio-economic system distorting the lives not only of the blacks who endured it — or who, like Jim, defied it — but of the whites who created and defended it. The final image of Southern society which Twain establishes is one of a profoundly corrupting and violent *milieu* in which few human virtues, such as simple loyalty to friends or respect for the lives of others, can survive. Those that do succeed do so only at great personal cost to individuals: Harney Shepherdson and Sophia Grangerford see their families wiped out, Huck is compelled to accept social death for most of the action, Jim has to give himself up into slavery so that Tom may live. The insistent gloom is the locus of all the forces contesting these qualities, the place where all the betrayals, squalid deaths (like Pap Finn's) and human degeneracy are situated. And it is the source, perhaps above all, of the unendurable loneliness which the many characters repeatedly experience. Conrad's Decoud excepted, Huck is the loneliest figure in all fiction.

Not surprisingly, shipwrecks occur in the fog or at night — though it is possibly noteworthy that the most graphic wreck in *The Gilded Age* occurs in full daylight, indicating Twain's deeper intent in *Huckleberry Finn*. More overtly symbolic, the treachery and murder aboard the *Walter Scott* is plotted in the dark; and, deliberately as it seems to me, Huck first experiences his isolation on Jackson's Island 'when it was dark.' Later, when he and Jim are separated by the fog, Huck warns the reader: 'If you think it ain't dismal and lonesome out in the fog that way, by

41

yourself, in the night, you try it – you'll see.' The parentheses effectively stress the connecting threads at this point: Huck solitary, unsighted, in the dark. And then even when the fogs lift the nights are unnaturally obscure. They become 'grey and ruther thick' instead, 'which is the next meanest thing to fog. You can't tell the shape of the river, and you can't see no distance.'

At the same time the gloom has a narrative structural use, vividly uniting one end of the action to the other. The process relates to the close dialectical interactions between aspects of the plot we have already traced.

Huck's first adventure, like his last, takes place in an inky midnight concealing men from themselves. Slipping away with Tom from Aunt Polly's house in chapter two, Huck hides in the darkness while Jim, the negro slave, peers into the void demanding, 'Who dah?' Huck tells us: 'He listened some more; then he came tip-toeing down and stood right between us; we could a touched him, nearly.' Finally Jim sits down and 'stretched his legs out till one of them most touched mine'. Still the man sees nothing and Huck marvels at his sightlessness – 'and we all there so close together'. It seems unnecessary to labour Twain's repeated emphasis that black and white might, in their proximity, reach out and touch one another if they cared to. Later, on the raft, Huck and Jim experience continual contact: 'Lemme look at you, chile, lemme feel o' you. No, you ain' dead!' The change runs parallel to Huck's maturing politics. The earlier scene is, in one way, a caught and tableau-like image of Southern society and of white racist attitudes in particular, since Jim is merely blind but Huck and Tom – the poor white and the middle class white – consciously avoid him. Twain displays a characteristic skill in slipping the point home while inducing us to watch him do something else: laugh at Huck's itchy discomfort in the dark. It is another instance of Twain's humourless humour. In another way, and for a related purpose and in a strikingly similar narrative manner, this scene and its import direct us to the novel's strange and controversial conclusion.

By the story's end, as we have seen, Huck and Tom are engaged in a plot to liberate Jim. They are nigger stealing. The significance of this enterprise at the level of the novel's political purpose is drawn partly from the contrast with the opening. The point is that in the earlier encounter Tom had plotted to rope Jim to a tree; symbolically and actually to imprison him. Now it is true that Twain's seriousness, especially in the evasion chapters, is undercut by the gratuitous farce he felt driven to employ; nevertheless the structural and intellectual affinities the final sequence shares with the opening indicate the fundamental gravity of his endeavour.

In the scene in chapter two Huck and Tom remain silent and breathless for several minutes after Jim has tip-toed towards them and then sat down unknowingly between them. Presently the tired slave, hearing and seeing nothing further, begins to nod off. The boys gradually move away but 'When we was ten foot off, Tom whispered to me and wanted to tie Jim to the tree for fun; but I said no; he might wake up and make a disturbance, and then they'd find out I warn't in.' Even at this point Huck resists imprisoning Jim, though his motives are entirely selfish and pragmatic. Tom, of course, caught up in his mischievous fantasy world, is completely alienated from the negro, seeing him not as a man but as something to be toyed with. And in fact, although he takes Huck's advice, he cannot resist playing a silly little trick, slipping Jim's hat off and hanging it on a branch over his head.

By the novel's end, however, Tom has become, with Huck, the chief agent of the runaway slave's freedom. The surrounding darkness of course has become no less intense — nothing has altered fundamentally in the South and Twain wishes to stress the seriousness of his analysis. The situation he describes, despite the distracting burlesque which is apparently intended to allow the author to make his point while no one is looking, makes palpable the Marxian tenet that as an economic crisis deepens into a political one, sections of the ruling class begin to go over to the oppressed. As we will see, this is precisely the politico-economic background to *Huckleberry Finn*. If this sounds beyond Twain's abilities, let us remind ourselves that he was a profoundly political man who spoke out for organised labour, was strongly drawn to socialism and who, in 1887, wrote to W.D. Howells:

. . .How stunning are the changes which age makes in a man while he sleeps. When I finished Carlyle's *French Revolution* in 1871 I was a Girondin; every time I have read it since I have read it differently — being influenced and changed, little by

43

little, by life and environment (and Taine and St Simon): and now I lay the book down once more, and recognise that I am a Sansculotte! And not a pale, characterless Sansculotte but a Marat. Carlyle teaches no such gospel: so the change is in *me* — in my vision of the evidences.

(*The Portable Mark Twain*, pp. 766-7.)

By the novel's final chapters Huck of course, like Twain, has fully allied himself both spiritually and materially with Jim. We know from Twain's *Autobiography* that he was raised with Huck's racist attitudes and abandoned them with like difficulty. It is Tom's commitment, therefore, which is surprising, and Twain makes Huck comment on it repeatedly.

> I says:
> 'All right; but wait a minute. There's one more thing — a thing that *nobody* don't know but me. And that is, there's a nigger here that I'm trying to steal out of slavery — and his name is *Jim* — old Miss Watson's Jim.'
> He says:
> 'What! Why Jim is —'
> He stopped and went to studying. I says:
> '*I* know what you'll say. You'll say it's a dirty low-down business; but what if it is? — *I'm* low down; and I'm agoing to steal him, and I want you to keep mum and not let on. Will you?'
> His eye lit up and he says:
> 'I'll *help* you steal him!'
> Well, I let go all holts then, like I was shot. It was the most astonishing speech I ever heard — and I'm bound to say Tom Sawyer fell, considerable, in my estimation. Tom Sawyer a *nigger stealer*!

(*Huckleberry Finn*, Chapter 33.)

Of course the situation is more complicated than this as we later discover. But what we need to stress here is that these last chapters are clearly calculated, at an important level, to be taken very seriously. Huck feels contempt for Tom because his consciousness, like Jim's, is still dominated by the perverted intellectual habits of Southern racism. It is both a fine insight on Twain's part and a further piece in the

44

developing mosaic of Huck's complex personality.

At the same time Twain's persistent black imagery suggests the weight he attached to the final sequence. All the preparations for the evasion are carried out at night, and the climactic moments occur in a darkness so profound that even the three escapees, as they have become, are hidden from one another:

> 'Hurry! *hurry*!' I says. 'Where's Jim?'
>
> 'Right at your elbow; if you reach out your arm you can touch him.'
>
> (Huckleberry Finn, Chapter 40.)

This deliberate echo of the opening episode seems both obvious and calculated to resonate on a deeper level than the literal. The enveloping gloom now, however, is a mutual ally and no longer only an interposition between friends. It is the armed slave-owners, bent on murder to defend their crumbling system, who are lost in the darkness. They have chained Jim to a bed and sealed him in a wood-shed; now in the dark they fumble with its padlock and stumble over the furniture. Amazingly – the detail is so telling that it cannot be a mere oversight on Twain's part – they have failed to bring a lantern or a torch with them. They can see nothing. The Phelpses and their allies are so alienated from their fellow humans they almost literally trample them underfoot, totally unaware of what they are doing. Twain's stress here is quite specific, his meaning limpid: 'So in they come, but couldn't see us in the dark, and most trod on us whilst we was hustling to get under the bed.'

In the adjoining lean-to Tom squints through a crack but can see nothing of their pursuers because of the dark. Twain's point is that it is not only interiors that are impenetrable; the outer night is obscured as well. 'Tom. . .put his eye to the crack, but couldn't make out nothing, it was so dark.' It is only when the evaders break for cover that they are glimpsed briefly. A shot is fired, Tom is wounded. After that the thick, light-consuming gloom swallows them up again.

Twain's purpose is to force upon the careful reader a comparison of his opening and closing, the direct parallels he establishes compelling an emphasis both on similarities and divergences. The earlier episode dramatised the barriers between Jim on the one hand and Tom and Huck on the other. By the end of the novel, however, where the same themes of darkness, ignorance and imprisonment/liberty are employed, the circumstances have altered radically. We now observe a poor white child and a boy from a middle-class white family effectively engaged in social subversion. This movement, which at the same time draws attention to the novel's dialectical unity, is both significant and pointed within the work's overall political impact.

3

Twain's Fiction and the Reading Public

For whom does one write? Sartre asks in the third section of *Qu'est-ce que la litterature*? (1948) and arrives at his celebrated Baudelairian formula of 'the double simultaneous postulation' (*la double postulation simultanee*).[1] This awkwardly translated phrase contains the notion of a split or fractured readership, two public foci, simultaneously but unequally addressed by the author. Both audiences, though reacting to and receiving the work separately, are nevertheless dialectically linked because of the nature of their responses and in the antagonisms inherent in their class positions. The successful modern writer is thus, according to Sartre, able synchronistically to retain the existence of the fracture − in a word, to exploit it − and make it the *occasion* for his short story or novel. (Sartre specifically excludes poetry from his analysis.) 'It is not that he is not aiming through them at all men,' he writes, 'but it is *through them* that he is thus aiming.' The modern writer takes advantage of the disjunction in order to transcend it.

Sartre illustrates his argument with the case of Richard Wright, a contemporary Black American novelist whose work peculiarly complements Twain's. Wright details the Southern experience from a black perspective, Twain from a white. Sartre's point, however, is that the fecund complexity of Wright's work arises directly from the fact that his readers are not his fictional subject − 'there are no clerks among the oppressed' − nor yet is he concerned to

---

[1]   Sartre's reference is to Baudelaire's posthumous *Journaux Intimes*, XIX: *'Il y a dans tout homme, à tout heure, deux postulations simultanées, l'un vers Dieu, l'autre vers Satan*.' Norbert Guterman renders this: 'Every man at every moment has two simultaneous tendencies, one toward God, the other toward Satan.' Baudelaire adds: *'L'invocation à Dieu, ou spiritualité, est un desir de menter en grade; celle de Satan, ou animalité, est un joie de descendre.'* Bernard Frechtman, translator of *What is Literature*? (London: Methuen, 1967) is thus being too literal in rendering as 'postulation' a word which has, in the French, overtones of demand, request, claim and solicitation.

47

address some vague abstraction such as the Universal Reader. (It might be argued that a novelist like Henry James represents Wright's antithesis, placing his readership at the centre of his fiction and addressing through them an idealised posterity.) But can Wright be intending his books 'for the white racists of Virginia or South Carolina whose minds are made up in advance and will not open them'? Can he seriously be thinking of writing for 'the black peasants of the bayous who cannot read'? And, Sartre adds, 'it is obvious that. . . he had not the slightest idea of writing for the European public' or some other audience in Asia, Africa, or India.

> These considerations are enough to define his readers. He is addressing himself to the cultivated negroes of the North and the white Americans of goodwill (intellectuals, democrats of the left, radicals, C.I.O. workers).
>
> (*What is Literature?* London, 1967, p. 58.)

Yet this is an inherently dichotomous audience. The northern blacks, on the one hand, represent what Sartre calls Wright's *subjective* public. They share his cultural perspectives and life experiences: not of course in the narrow individual sense, but in a common awareness of the condition of the race, of its *situation*. Wright mediates between them and their history, not only by articulating the particular and giving it artistic point, but in the very act of literary creation itself. 'He is their conscience, and the movement by which he raises himself from the immediate to the reflective capturing of his condition is that of the whole race.'

The white, on the other hand, are Wright's objective readers, though Sartre avoids using this term. They are, he says, the *Other*. Their understanding of the negro world is inferential, analogical, even metaphorical; and, equally, Wright's perception of them *qua* audience is unsure and incomplete. Each necessarily — the predicament arises from the fact that both sides are allotropically situated — regards the other from without.

The problem is most acute for the literary artist, since he cannot know and can only partly guess at the resonances and associations his words will generate in their minds. Yet clearly he wishes to act upon them — to appeal, as Sartre expresses it elsewhere, to their freedom. This only then is certain, that the class, race and social circumstances of his white readership will of itself transform and modify his work so that, for them, its whole meaning is altered and transfigured. Where Wright speaks for and to his fellow blacks, acting both as witness and prophet, 'it is a matter of implicating [his white readers] and making them take stock of their responsibilities. He must make them indignant and ashamed.' Thus Sartre arrives at his central point, formulating the double simultaneous postulation, in which each word written by the novelist

> refers to two contexts; two forces are applied simultaneously to each phrase and determine the incomparable tension of his tale. Had he spoken to the whites alone, he might have turned out to be more prolix, more didactic, and more abusive; to the negroes alone, still more elliptical, more of a confederate, and more elegiac. In the first case, his work might have come close to satire; in the second, to prophetic lamentations. Jeremiah spoke only to the Jews. But Wright, a writer for a split public, has been able both to maintain and go beyond this split. He has made it the pretext for a work of art.

(What is Literature? p. 59.)

These ideas may clarify a central critical dilemma posed by *Huckleberry Finn*, namely the uneasy oscillations between levels of artistic achievement we detailed in the previous section. Twain, the detribalised Southern white, abandons in his closing chapters the stylistic richness and invention rising from the ambivalent public focus of most of the rest of the novel, collapsing in a little heap of grotesque social genuflection and narrative trivia. The crucial difference between Twain and Wright is that, at least in the unsuccessful portions of *Huckleberry Finn*, the literary fecundity coming from the fact of a dual audience abruptly, but explicably, ceases. The reason is that the double simultaneous postulate has been given up. In the final analysis Twain sells Jim, Huck and his novel down the river. He becomes Miss Watson.

Who are Twain's audiences? Certainly not the blacks either of the north or of the south. Despite Jim's moving dignity and sound pragmatic judgment in the novel's mid-section he remains, as Ellison remarked, a white man's inadequate portrait of a slave. His moral and intellectual degeneration in the Phelps episode, together with the way blacks as a group are treated in the novel, puts the point beyond contention. Ellison, we recall, could identify with Huck but not with Jim; in my experience this is a common reaction among black readers. And at the same time — this is the obverse of the argument — Jim is consistently portrayed, in his superior capacities, as an *exception*. The black racial norm in *Huckleberry Finn* is represented by the passive, yassuh-nossuh cardboard samboes who wait hand and foot upon their white betters in the Grangerford, Wilks and Phelps sequences; it is finally exemplified in Jim's wooly-haired jailer, nigger Nat, who wears charms in his peppercorn curls to ward off evil spirits and who can't tell eleven real dogs from one imaginary devil. And of course he knows his place; when an adolescent white boy invents a fantastic story about witch's pie and then offers to make one, Nat's reaction is: 'Will you do it, honey? — will you? I'll wasshup do groun' und' yo' foot, I will!'[1]

Twain's subjective readership then is clearly white, and Southern. Yet his focus is sharper still than this, as the following passage demonstrates:

> When him and the old lady come down in the morning, all the family got up out of their chairs and give them good-day, and didn't set down again till they had set down. Then Tom and Bob went to the sideboard where the decanters was, and mixed a glass of bitters and handed it to him, and he held it in his hand and waited till Tom's and Bob's was mixed, and then they bowed and said 'Our duty to you, sir, and madam;' and they bowed the least bit in the world and said thank you, and so they drank, all three and Bob and Tom poured a spoonful of water on the sugar and the mite of whisky or apple brandy in the bottom of their tumblers, and give it to me and Buck, and we drank to the old people too.

(*Huckleberry Finn*, Chapter 18.)

[1] I am grateful to Lewis Smith for pointing out that, despite Twain's pride in depicting 'the Missouri negro dialect,' black speech in the novel is not accurately rendered. Twain largely limits himself to the basic phonemic differences between black and conventional dialects, especially the substitution of the 'd' phoneme for the standard 'th', ignoring such complexities in black speech as immediate and continuous aspect, the distribution of plural markers in modifiers, and the zero relative pronoun. (Lewis Smith, unpublished paper given before the Radical Caucus of the M.L.A, 1973.) For a discussion of black dialect see Eugene D. Genovese: *Roll, Jordan, Roll* (New York, 1974) pp. 431-41, and J.L. Dillard: *Black English* (New York, 1972).

It is the Grangerford family breaking their fast in the morning. Huck's faint amusement at the absurd ritual, the distance he places between ourselves and them by his conscientious detailing of the ceremony *as* ceremony (the connectives, then. . .and. . .and), indicates both the class differentiation and the variance from the implicit social norm which is the novel's primary focus. This is an upper-bourgeois world; it is sexist (only the men drink); and it is faintly hypocritical. The Grangerfords are the aristocracy of Huckleberry's society; it is not for them and their kind — the Shepherdsons and Colonel Sherburn — that this book is written. Huck is a visitor in their midst and he reports back to us — that is, to Twain's subjective reading public — both on the curious style of their life and, finally, upon the manner of their death.

But if Twain is not writing for the cultivated upper bourgeoisie of the wealthy South, *the quality* as Huck calls them, equally is he unconcerned with the small-town poor and unemployed working class. In Pokeville — the name is of course satirical and pointed — Huck depicts the grubby boredom of Southern village life. His eye, Twain's eye, is all for local colour and low comedy. The men — 'loafers' — lounge about the main street yawning, scratching, whittling, waiting for something to happen. They are 'a mighty ornery lot' whose world is limited to tobacco, dog fights and 'considerable many cuss-words'. Twain is really caught up in the patronising activity of depicting the supposed life-style and speech of one class for the amused edification of another:

'Gimme a chaw'v tobacker, Hank.'

'Cain't — I hain't got but one chaw left. Ask Bill.'

Maybe Bill he gives him a chaw; maybe he lies and says he ain't got none. Some of them kinds of loafers never has a cent in the world, nor a chaw of tobacco of their own. They get all their chawing by borrowing — they say to a fellow, 'I wisht you'd len' me a chaw, Jack, I jist this minute give Ben Thompson the last chaw I had' — which is a lie, pretty much every time; it don't fool nobody but a stranger; but Jack ain't no stranger, so he says;

'*You* give him a chaw, did you? so did your sister's cat's grandmother. You pay me back the chaws you've awready borry'd off'n me, Lafe Buckner, then I'll loan you one or two ton of it, and won't charge you back no intrust, nuther.'

'Well, I *did* pay you back some of it wunst.'

51

'Yes, you did — 'bout six chaws. You borry'd store tobacker and paid back nigger-head.'

Store tobacco is flat black plug, but these fellows mostly
chaws the natural leaf twisted. When they borrow a chaw, they
don't generly cut it off with a knife, but they set the plug
between their teeth, and gnaw with their teeth and tug at the
plug with their hands till they get it in two — then sometimes
the one that owns the tobacco looks mournful at it when it's
handed back, and says, sarcastic —

'Here, gimme the *chaw*, and you take the *plug*.'

(*Huckleberry Finn*, Chapter 21.)

The last paragraph is the give-away, Twain in action as amateur
sociologist and class emissary to the lower orders. The other tell-
tale is his use of eye-dialect — 'awready' — the visual rendering of
class speech calculated to evoke a smile. And moreover Twain
permits both this, and the total thrust of the passage, to take place
at the cost of considerable violence to Huck, the ostensible narrator, who is here shown aping a spurious gentility (he pronounces
tobacco correctly) by looking down on the penury of others. In
other words, this is not really Huck's voice at all, but Twain's.

It becomes apparent that Twain's subjective public is the social
class situated midway between the excessively grand, ceremonious
and violent Grangerfords, and the reprehensibly poor and lazy
village lay-abouts. That is, we are talking about the petty-bourgeoisie of the ante-bellum South — the world of white Hannibal
and the small plantation owners like the Phelpses who were their
rural analogy. This was of course Twain's own class *milieu;*
compare, for instance, this description of his uncle's tobacco
plantation near Florida, Missouri, where Twain was born, and
which he visited regularly in his boyhood. Clearly they are the
same place, as indeed Twain acknowledged: [1]

[1] 'I have never consciously used [my uncle, John A. Quarles] or his wife
in a book, but his farm has come very handy to me in literature once or
twice. In *Huck Finn* and in *Tom Sawyer, Detective* I moved it down to
Arkansas. It was all of six hundred miles, but it was no trouble; it was not
a very large farm — five hundred acres, perhaps — but I could have done it
If it had been twice as large. And as for the morality of it, I cared nothing for
that; I would move a state if the exigencies of literature required it.'

(*Mark Twain's Autobiography*, p. 96.)

The farmhouse stood in the middle of a very large yard, and the yard was fenced on three sides with rails and on the rear side with high palings; against these stood the smoke-house; beyond the palings was the orchard; beyond the orchard were the negro quarters and the tobacco fields. The front yard was entered over a stile made of sawed-off logs of graduated heights; I do not remember any gate. In a corner of the front yard were a dozen lofty hickory trees and a dozen black walnuts; and in the nutting season riches were to be gathered there.

Down a piece, abreast of the house, stood a little log cabin against the rail fence; and there the woody hill fell sharply away, past the barns, the corn-crib, the stables, and the tobacco-curing house, to a limpid brook. . .

(*Mark Twain's Autobiography*, pp. 98-99.)

Phelps's was one of these little one-horse cotton plantations; and they all look alike. A rail fence round a two-acre yard; a stile, made of logs sawed off and up-ended, in steps, like barrels of a different length, to climb over the fence with, and for women to stand on when they are going to jump onto a horse; some sickly grass-patches in the big yard, but mostly it was bare and smooth, like an old hat with the nap rubbed off; big double log house for the white folks — hewed logs, with the chinks stopped up with mud or mortar, and these mud-stripes been whitewashed some time or another; round-log kitchen, with big broad, open but roofed passage joining it to the house; log smoke-house back of the kitchen; three little log nigger cabins in a row t'other side of the smoke-house; one little hut all by itself away against the back fence, and some out-buildings down a piece the other side; ash-hopper, and big kettle to bile soap in, by a little hut; bench by the kitchen door, with bucket of water and gourd; hound asleep there, in the sun; more hounds asleep, round about; about three shade-trees away off in a corner; some currant bushes and gooseberry bushes in one place by the fence; outside the fence a garden and water-melon patch; then the cotton fields begins; and after the fields, the woods.

(*Huckleberry Finn*, Chapter 32.)

One of Twain's objectives in writing the novel was to give, for the first time, definition to the hitherto undefined in literary art:

his own social class, the white inhabitants of the small Southern rural farms and their equivalents in the neighbouring towns. And of course he succeeded brilliantly; in the end, perhaps, this is his major achievement in *Huckleberry Finn*.

Like Richard Wright, Twain was his people's conscience and its voice. *Conscience:* Sartre slices to the essence of the matter with this word. Twain's attempt to define his *milieu*, like Ibsen's or T.S. Eliot's, was not always welcomed since, like all great writers, he was not interested in giving back to his uncle John Quarles, for example, merely his own reflection. Twain's is a critical account of his late petty-bourgeois world; he repeatedly attacks what he took to be its backwardness in such matters as religion, politics and the hypocrisy of public attitudes. But he loves it nonetheless; and thus, though he speaks from an external vantage, conscience is the precise characterisation to employ. And *voice*: above all, Twain is the fond historian of this peculiar outpost of Anglo-Saxon society. Beyond its obvious failures *Huckleberry Finn* remains a great social document, an act of profound historical witness, produced at first hand by an intelligent and sensitive man who had been there. If our conclusion is that *Huckleberry Finn* is ultimately a subversive novel, that is because, as Jorge Semprun has observed, the truth is always so. ('Socialism and Literature', *Radical Perspectives in the Arts*, Ed. Baxandall, London, 1972, p. 201.)

The Other, Twain's objective readership, is defined with greater ease, since it was embodied both literally and figuratively in the person of Twain's wealthy but ailing wife, Olivia Langdon Clemens. The romantic story of their courtship and marriage is well known: how Twain chanced to meet her brother, Charles Langdon, when they were both passengers on board the *Quaker City* to Europe and the Holy Land in 1867 – the tour Twain described in his first literary success, *The Innocents Abroad* (1869); how the young journalist fell in love with the little portrait of Livy which Charles always carried; how he pressed and pressed for an introduction and finally met her that Christmas, after returning to the States; and how the two were at last married early in 1870, despite the opposition of her family.

But was it really love at first sight of a miniature for the thirty-three year-old Twain? – he who had grown up along the Mississippi, deserted westwards from the Confederate army and prospected for silver in Nevada? Livy's portrait actually reveals a rather

54

severe and plain-looking woman who, even according to those who loved her, including Twain, was equipped with a personality to match. The word 'tyrant' was never far away in his letters about her. In addition she had been permanently invalided since the age of sixteen. Thus, despite the rather odd remark Twain made much later in life, humorously referring to those strange men who do not experience sexual intercourse until they are thirty-five, one cannot help the sense that the whole pretty story is redolent with the hypocrisies of Victorian sentiment. The truth was more probably that, like Forster's Helen Schlegel, he had fallen in love not with an individual, but a family. *Nel mezzo del cammin di nostra vita* was a rather late age for adolescence, even in the nineteenth century.

Because the fact was that Livy had other advantages beyond her immediate person. She was one of the New York Langdons, a rich and powerful and well-connected family headed by Jervis Langdon, a wealthy coal mine owner and philanthropist. Livy was his only daughter. Twain, on the other hand, was an obscure, red-haired Southern journalist whose origins, according to the prejudices of the New England bourgeoisie, were highly dubious. The prospect of his marrying into the Langdons sent a collective shudder through them: he was, at best, 'this novel. . .Westerner', as Mrs Thomas Aldrich called him. Samuel Langhorn Clemens was precisely not the sort of man Jervis Langdon wanted for a son-in-law, and at an early stage he forbade Twain to see his daughter again. It was only the young man's persistence that won through in the end.

Obviously, what made Twain impossible for the Langdons made Livy intensely desirable for Twain. Soon after meeting her for the first time he wrote to his friend, Mrs ('Mother') Fairbanks, describing her in terms whose class and sexual sonics are almost infinite. That is, Livy's attraction for him lay precisely in her upper-class background — a kind of slumming in reverse. 'There isn't much of her', Twain confessed, 'but what there is assays as high as any bullion I ever saw.' Where he was dross, she was gold; where he was large and crude, she was small and fine. Where he swore, she was demure; where he drank and smoked freely — but in private — she was temperate; where he was virile and voluble and full of robust health, she was quiet, restrained and of course physically frail. Her frailty was part of her value; Twain could play

Robert Browning to her Elizabeth. Her weakness supposedly balanced his provinciality: Twain compared her self-consciousness of it to his embarrassment over his regional accent. He wrote to Mrs Fairbanks: 'Livy is no stronger than she was six months ago — and it seems hard and grieves me to have to say it. I cannot talk about it with her. . .for she is as sensitive about it as I am about my drawling speech, and stammerers of their infirmity. She turns *crimson* when it is mentioned, and it hurts her worse than a blow . . .She is a small tyrant, physically, but a powerful one when she chooses to let herself go'. (Harnsberger: *Mark Twain: Family Man*, New York, 1960, p.55)

In short, Livy was a Lady, which means an upper-class woman. Her 'breeding' — that is, her socially-privileged origin — was her most marked characteristic. To her friends she was 'an exquisite lily', and 'the flower and perfume of ladylikeness'. Mrs Aldrich recalled of 'this white and fragile flower' that 'the men of her world said, 'We did not dare to speak of love to her, she seemed as if she so lightly touched the earth, belonging to another sphere.' W.D. Howells, who became a close friend of the Clemenses after their move to Hartford in 1871, repeatedly praised Livy's social grace and refinement — metaphors for knowledge of middle class manners and rituals. Only Samuel Clemens was bold enough to face down Jervis Langdon and woo his wilting flower of a girl.

Unquestionably, the marriage was overwhelmingly advantageous to Twain. Beyond literary success he had two great ambitions: financial security and acceptance into the East coast establishment. Livy provided him with the last two; the first would come in time. At a stroke his marriage swept him among the very thickets of the New England middle class, and placed undreamed of riches immediately at his finger ends. Among Jervis's first actions after the marriage was establishing his son-in-law in a spanking new home in Buffalo, New York, equipped with stable, horses and carriage, and buying him a third interest in the *Buffalo Express* together with the literary editorship of the paper. Even by modern standards Jervis's outlay is impressive: $40,000 for the home, $25,000 for the job. Clearly he felt that if Livy was intent on marrying this boor, he should do what he could to raise the fellow from the gutter. And Twain hardly demurred, but accepted what was offered with alacrity.

With alacrity, but also, after a while, with misgivings. In Buffalo he quickly came face to face with the sterility of bourgeois comforts. 'Behold then Samuel L. Clemens', he wrote, '– now become for everybody Mark Twain, the great American humorist – the rough days of his western life put behind him, settled down at number 472 Delaware Avenue, Buffalo, trying hard to be respectable. Here he lives the model life of a family man, joins in morning prayer and listens as best he can to the daily reading of the Scriptures. More than that, he even makes desperate efforts to give up smoking. He has his wife at his side, his desk at his elbow, and the world at his feet. After all, what does tobacco matter? Let's have another chapter of Deuteronomy.' (Foner: *Mark Twain: Social Critic*, New York, 1958, p.172.)

Twain's sense of dislocation went to the heart of his new existence: indeed, the felt class differential between himself and Livy was the chief reference point in all his dealings with the Langdons. It defined his relationship with them. 'When I am permanently *settled*', he had written in the early days of his courtship, '– and when I am a Christian – and when I have *demonstrated* that I have a good, steady, reliable character, her parents will withdraw their objections. . .' (Wecter (ed): *The Love Letters of Mark Twain*, New York, 1949, p.97.) In other words, when he had assimilated their middle class virtues. Twain's petty-bourgeois origins and manners were a matter of contempt with the Langdons before his marriage, and a matter of genial contempt with them after it. On one occasion Jervis, with the icy kindliness so characteristic of an upper-class insult, even offered Twain money to give up smoking. The scarcely-veiled suggestion that if his son-in-law could not be educated he might at least be bought, was not lost on those concerned.

At the same time the balance of forces within his marriage, including his subsequent relationship with his daughters, pivoted on the emphasised contrast between his lowly origins and supposed roughness, and their upper-class life-style. It was a question, as Clara Clemens later expressed it, 'of dusting papa off'. He was of the grubby pathways of common life while they were – Langdons. Sam was the village ruffian – Huck Finn, in fact – and Aunt Livy was going to 'sivilise' him.

Bringing Up Father was the chief strategy the Clemenses

employed to deal with the embarrassing fact that Livy had married beneath herself. The other but lesser ploy was the elaborate fiction of Twain's unbridled passion and their romantic, fairy-tale courtship. Twain himself entered into both with spirit, on the one hand repeating the tale of his great love, on the other delighting in playing Beast to Livy's Beauty, Caliban to her Miranda. Both games were played with stern zest as though to prove they were, after all, only games. Among his immediate family Twain was considered amusingly low and vulgar; and of course he had to be clucked at and reproved. But both sides were ambiguous about the situation. Twain at bottom longed to be a gentleman, or at east to be accepted as such, but sensed that the pressure to uproot his habits was crushing his individuality and creativity. Livy on the other hand was genuinely appalled by his rudeness and impiety, but was drawn to his vitality and virility. It was a very Victorian marriage, involving the kind of disposition of forces to which a writer such as Lawrence would later obsessively recur.

Their relationship — in many ways an upper-class version of the Morels' — became a protracted struggle by Livy to save her unregenerate husband from his lower impulses — drinking, smoking, swearing. Small victories would be followed by larger defeats; of course neither side was intended to win. Livy's campaigns — some lasted for more than ten years — were always projected in moral terms. There seems to have been little comprehension that she was really presenting the mores of her class in ethical-religious dress. And for a while, especially in the early years of their marriage, Twain went along, hypocritically mumbling grace into his porridge and sneaking a quick cigar and whiskey in the bath-tub. Livy was what he called, with metaphorically uprolled eyes, his 'Better Way,' an 'angel' who would bring him salvation (both religious and social). 'I was a mighty rough, coarse, unpromising subject when Livy took charge of me 4 years ago', he wrote in 1874, 'and I may *still* be, to the rest of the world, but not to her. She has made a very creditable job of me.'

The image of the rough-hewn diamond or unfinished art-work is not far below the surface in this statement. Twain was the raw material, but Livy worked him into something acceptable to the New England middle class. The significance of this far from unique circumstance is that Twain allowed Livy to extend the principle to his work. She was given the same decisive power over his fiction.

The next important moment in Sam Clemens's progress from Southern Untouchable to East Coast Brahmin took place in 1871 when he, now Mark Twain (Langdon), gave up his position with the *Buffalo Express* and moved his family to Hartford, Connecticut. At that time the city was one of the centres of middle class intellectuality – the final bastion. To be accepted by the New England elite – this was, as Bret Harte once told Howells, 'the dream of Mark's life:'. Twain set about achieving his goal with characteristic resolution. Drawing without hesitation on Livy's fortune, he built himself a vast and showy mansion in Hartford's most respectable area – he, who only a few years before, had visited the city in penury to report back to his paper about the wealth and luxuriousness of the dwellings there. Twain's Hartford home, built to his own extraordinary specifications, instantly became the most talked about building in the town; news of it spread even to London. The luxury of its appointments, and the fantastic details drawn from the architecture of Mississippi steamers which Twain insisted on including (a pilot house, a deck, etc.) together with the lavishness with which the Clemenses entertained, won them instant admission to the innermost circles of the intellectual community. If Twain had had any hesitations about bourgeois life in Buffalo his move to Hartford hardly reflected them.

Almost as soon as they arrived in town the Clemenses were adopted by the Bloomsbury-like world of the Nook Farm Circle: a small, selfconsciously elite cluster of middle-class writers and thinkers. At the centre of the group was Harriet Beecher Stowe, the Virginia Woolf of her world; among her close associates was Charles Dudley Warner (whom Twain, in a significant gesture of self-assimilation, invited to collaborate with him on *The Gilded Age* (1873); the Reverend Joseph ('Joe') Twichell, who came to exercise almost as decisive an influence over Twain's work as Livy; W.D. Howells; and lesser persons such as Thomas and Isabella Hooker (an ardent feminist), George Warner (Charles's brother), and Mrs Frances Gilette and her son, William. Contemporaries viewed the circle as somewhat Bohemian; they were said to visit one another's homes without the elaborate formality expected of the upper classes (calling cards, butlers, Mrs So-and-so regrets to say she is not at home, etc.), and were rumoured to have rather liberal political views. Mrs Stowe, after all, was the author of *Uncle Tom's Cabin*. Mark Twain, who was later to produce the most radical of their writings, *A Connecticut Yankee in King Arthur's Court* (1889), rapidly won the reputation of being the most eccentric of the lot.

The Clemenses' new home outrageously and deliberately procc-claimed the wealth and social status of its occupants. It was, in its showy display of conspicuous consumption and waste, the perfect illustrations of Veblen's theory of the leisure class. At a time when economic depression was eating into income, Twain spent more than $120,000 on his mansion without even looking back. The *Hartford Times* reported that it was equipped with 'numerous bathrooms. . .no less than five balconies' and, on the west side, with an 'octagonal tower 62 feet 4 inches in height' and lesser towers on the north and south sides. Persian carpets littered the floor in ostensibly careless profusion, rich oriental hangings bed-ecked the walls and widows, specially imported sculptures and paintings from France and Italy surmounted the library doors, the armchairs, the expensive couches. To maintain this splendour the Clemenses employed more than half a dozen servants, including a butler, a cook, a housemaid, a laundress, a nurse for the children and, of course, a coachman to drive the horses when they visited their friends. Money was rarely an object in the Clemens' home; the combined annual salary of the servants was colossal. And on one occasion Livy, seized by an impulse, ordered the complete redesign of the washroom bowls so that they would 'harmonise' with the rugs in the adjoining halls.

But Twain remained torn by the contradictions built into his class origins and the style of life he was supposed to become accustomed to. The very architecture of his Hartford home revealed the paradox at the centre of his personality and marriage: the awkwardly reconciled elements of steamboat and middle class establishment. He himself, in a revealing comment, described the house as part Mississippi steamboat, part medieval stronghold and part cuckoo clock (which it is): suggesting that he was conscious at least in some measure of the rending and division. He was after all, twain.

In an immediate and very real sense, then, the Nook Farm com-munity was Twain's Other audience, his objective public. The very first book he sat down to write after coming to Hartford indicates the nature of the split: *Roughing It* (1872). The book was subtitled *The Innocents At Home*: in other words, detailing for one readership (Livy-Twichell) the experiences of another (the Southern white — himself). But it was projected, of course, in upper-bourgeois terms. The titling alone suggests the implicit standards of comfort and shelter at issue. Its contents — Twain's overland journey to Carson City and his adventures among the silver miners in Nevada — made the point explicit.

Livy on this occasion and always thereafter until her death was her husband's critical lodestar. Everything he wrote he willingly subjected to her censure and censorship, and she exercised her power freely. The analogy between this situation and the control Livy exerted within the home is obvious. At the same time, the existence of this extraordinary literary relationship is well known; it has been repeatedly detailed by others and thus no purpose would be served in my reploughing old ground. What seems never to have been fully drawn, however, are the full implications of Livy's critical dominance. She was the voice of her class, and her blue pencil the colour of its prejudices. Van Wyk Brooks, in one of the many fine studies dealing (in part) with the influence of Livy on Sam, cites a memorandum Twain made at the time when she and he were going over the proofs of *Following the Equator* (1897). Cast in disalogue form, it reveals not only the manner of Livy's tyranny but Twain's uneasy acquiescence. Again, the paradox of his bifurcated readership becomes apparent.

Page 1, 020, 9th line from the top. I think some other word would be better than 'stench.' You have used that pretty often.

But can't I get it in anywhere? You've knocked it out every time. Out it goes again. And yet 'stench' is a noble, good word.

Page 1,038. I hate to have your father pictured as lashing a slave boy.

It's out, and my father is whitewashed.

Page 1,050, 2nd line from the bottom.Change 'breechclout.' It's a word that you love and I abominate. I would take that and 'offal' out of the language.

You are steadily weakening the English tongue, Livy.
(The Ordeal of Mark Twain, New York, 1920, p.68).

Brooks makes rather too much of this complaint. To savour the full ambiguity of Twain's situation we have to balance his memorandum with other evidence, like this testimony from his daughter Clara:

How often did my father express his gratitude to the marvellous fate that had given him such a companion, one who was as deeply absorbed in his work as he was himself! One who had a pure instinct for the correct balance of values in literature as well as in life, and one whose adverse criticism proved invariably to be a just criticism because her intuition — born of a large heart and mind — hit the target plumb in the centre.

(Harnsberger: *Mark Twain: Family Man*, p. 59.)

The revealing part of this observation, for our purposes, lies in Clara's easy linkage of literature and life. Obviously she is reflecting the scant distinction between the two, so far as Livy's critical function·was concerned, her father himself drew. Further, we can justly infer that Livy's 'intuition' for the 'correct balance of values' points to both the manner and content of her prescriptive disapprovals, and the class standards she clearly must have brought to bear. Clara thus unconsciously lays the situation open to its essence: the literary and social deracination of America's first great petty-bourgeois novelist.

And yet of course the process was far from absolute. Twain alternately placated and outraged his wife, both as a man and as a novelist. He permitted just so much interference; then he drew the line. A well-known anecdote, for instance, has Twain warning Livy that there will be no censoring of his autobiography. On that occasion at least, he told her, all the truth would be told, without varnish or concealment.

And his autobiography is the less interesting because of it. The book's value lies in the fact that it comes from the hand of a major novelist; as a work it is occasionally dull, prolix and, in the passages dealing with Twain's children, often maudlin. Livy *was* a significant critical presence in her husband's fiction, though not in the way she or he understood. At its best the force of her social prejudices wrought the creative tension we have identified as Twain's greatest narrative strength. The fact of Livy made it possible for him to define, however unconsciously, his other audience. And as long as he kept both readerships in view, again no matter how unconsciously, Twain was able to produce some of the finest literary art of his epoch.

But, on the other hand, the arrangement finally destroyed him as a novelist — though never was writer more willingly dispatched. On the merely material level, Twain's access to riches brought about his eventual bankruptcy through repeatedly misguided investments in all manner of unworkable patents. (The one invention Twain did turn down was offered by the young Alexander Graham Bell.) This situation led to his now-forgotten pot-boilers and famous humorous readings on the lecture-circuit. At a deeper level, however, the oppressive presence of Livy's judgment corrupted his fiction from within. The collapse of *Huckleberry Finn* exemplifies the process: the evasion chapters are the merest titillations of the Nook Farm mentality. It is no coincidence that it was precisely from these sequences that Twain, in his later years on the public platform, chose to read. He knew, perhaps unconsciously, that they presented the image of the South most valued by his Northern and European audiences. Again, it is no mere chance that W.D. Howells, in a complex recognition of Twain's double role as campaigner-against-slavery and spokesman for the Northern middle class, compared him to Lincoln – 'he is the Lincoln of our literature.' It was when Twain snapped the creative tension in his work by discarding one of its poles – the subjective, Southern petty-bourgeoisie – that his writing collapsed in the rubble of his final years.

Huckleberry Finn displays Twain at the cross-roads. In its great sections and sequences the novel transcends the split readership, making it, as Sartre argued for *Native Son*, the occasion for a magnificent piece of fiction. Twain never addresses his subjective audience in isolation from the Other; this is why the best parts of the book – the journey down river, the Grangerford chapters, most of the Wilks story, Huck's relationship with Jim and the whole background of disintegrating slavery – are never couched in terms of 'lamentation or false prophecy'. Always Twain brings a keen intellectual cutting-edge to bear in his analysis, a stringency and rough humour that, paradoxically, as we have seen, emphasises the serious nature of his concerns. The sources of his perspective were, of course, the positive and at time revolutionary values of the eighteenth and early-nineteenth century American bourgeoisie – the class that had exalted the common man, abhorred slavery, and held that truths about human equality and the responsibilities of governments were self-evident.

On the other hand Twain did, increasingly, address his other audience in isolation from the first. His second readership comprised the descendants of the original American revolutionary class, already beginning to sentimentalise their political heritage and edge towards conservatism and hypocrisy. Ten years earlier Twain had savagely attacked their dishonesties and double standards in *The Guilded Age*; by the time he came to write the later sections of *Huckleberry Finn*, however, he was merely their court-jester. This led, precisely as Sartre prophesied, to pale burlesque and satire. The weak humour in, for example, the duke's unconscious parody of Hamlet's soliloquy depends absolutely upon not only an educated knowledge of the original but a reasonably detailed acquaintance with the rest of Shakespeare. Twain is ignoring his subjective readers here entirely. He is at it again in the joke he milks from Huck's account of the European monarchies: it's the same sort of humour as *1066 and All That*. That is to say, to understand the jest you have to be educated yourself. You have to be W.D. Howells.

> Look at Henry the Eight; this'n's a Sunday-School Superintendant to *him*. And look at Charles Second, and Louis Fourteen, and Louis Fifteen, and James Second, and Richard Third and forty more; besides all them Saxon heptarchies that used to rip around in all times raising Cain. My, you ought to seen old Henry Eight when he was in bloom. He *was* a blossom. He used to marry a new wife every day, and chop off her head next morning. And he would do it just as indifferent as if he was ordering up eggs. 'Fetch up Nell Gwynn,' he says. They fetch her up. Next morning, 'Chop off her head!' And they chop it off. 'Fetch up Jane Shore,' he says: and up she comes. Next morning 'Chop off her head' – and they chop it off. 'Ring up Fair Rosamun.' Fair Rosamun answers the bell. Next morning, 'Chop off her head.' And he made every one of them tell him a tale every night; and he kept that up till he had hogged a thousand and one tales that way, and then he put them all in a book and called it Domesday Book – which was a good name and stated the case.

> *(Huckleberry Finn*, Chapter 23.)

Heptarchies! In the mouth of Huck Finn? The word is so out of character, so improbable, that the reader winces uneasily. He senses that Twain has abandoned his dual audience and has begun to flatter the Other through in-jokes and knowing winks over Huck's head. And thereafter, but especially of course in the evasion

64

chapters, Twain compounds his flattery with sycophancy. For that is what his complete adoption of the bourgeois perspective finally becomes. The real heroes of *Huckleberry Finn* are, precisely, the representatives of the educated bourgeoisie in St Petersburg, Pokeville and elsewhere along the river. They are Judge Thatcher; Dr Robinson and the Rev. Hobson – the only people at the Wilkses' able to see through the king and the duke; the anonymous kindly doctor who tends Tom at the Phelpses'; the new Miss Watson of the final revelation and – of course – Tom Sawyer. It is they who, finally, are allowed to project the implicit standards of normality and good conduct against which the book measures itself. It is they who, finally, set things right and aportion the appropriate rewards and punishments. It is their world. Intermittently at first, and then increasingly as the story develops, they are permitted to take over from Huck until he is entirely eclipsed and the book slithers towards its final period. This is why I said earlier Twain becomes Miss Watson. Perhaps I should have said Miss Langdon. The conclusion of *Huckleberry Finn* is Livy Clemens's pyrrhic triumph.

PART TWO

The Novelist as Historian

4

Racism, Slavery and Freedom

Can literature be historical evidence? The etymology of the word *fiction* suggests not. Yet it has been our argument that the artistic successes in *Huckleberry Finn* derive almost entirely from the accurately-observed detail and subversive politics which give the novel its characteristic texture and point of view. It is exactly when Twain begins obviously to distort and float free from the historically feasible — i.e., principally in the evasion chapters — that his story, by almost universal agreement, stumbles badly. Moreover, as we have seen, his failure as a writer at this point cannot be disentangled from his capacity to compromise and modify his original political critique. The prickly social satire of the early chapters becomes the blunt club of parody and burlesque by the end. At his best Twain was the perceptive and intelligent on-looker and in-looker who had been *there* — the pluperfect is a crucial part of this formulation — and who was able to record with integrity for both his subjective and objective readerships the particular circumstances producing the socio-political crisis which is the novel's heart. But at his worst he was merely a joker. He thus oscillates between what Lukács called 'radical objectivity' — the truthful and critical delineation of social fact from an identifiable Left perspective — and mere liberal opportunism.

These points will bear further scrutiny and illustration for at least two reasons. First, because I realise that my approach may be considered controversial. But secondly and more importantly, because it is finally my case that part of the novel's value for a twentieth century audience resides in the fidelity with which Twain depicted and then analysed the first disintegrating cracks in the edifice of Southern chattel slavery. And more, that he did this in the context and with the obvious intention of developing an overwhelming and unanswerable moral and political refutation of 'the peculiar institution'. As we shall see, the fact that he undertook this enterprise more than a decade after the official abolition of slavery was no mere whimsey. Those critics who query the novel's political stance on this basis quite miss the point. Eighteen seventy-six, the year in which Twain settled down to write *Huckleberry Finn*, was also the year in which the victorious Northern Republicans reached their historic political compromise with the Southern Democrats, effectively reintroducing white supremacy in the old Confederacy. All the civil libertarian gains of the War were thus in practise wiped out, and racism and *de facto* slavery were back on the national agenda. It was therefore vital, as Twain clearly perceived, that a contemporary indictment of the antebellum South must be immediately developed. The first two hundred pages of *Huckleberry Finn* was his response.[1]

At the same time, as we have already recognised, the novel was also an act of graceful tribute to a way of life which, although considered by Twain to have been profoundly anachronistic, was nevertheless almost equally profoundly loved by him. It is a divided work of fiction, and this is why its moods alternate between bursts of nostalgia and cynicism.

[1] Something of Twain's state of mind in 1876 can be gathered from his short tale, 'A True Story – Repeated Word for Word as I Heard it', written in that year. The narrator is 'Aunt Rachel,' an elderly ex-slave in the author's service, who gives a moving account of her life. The central episode tells of the forcible break-up of her family on the auction block – the aspect of chattel slavery which, as we see in more detail below appalled Twain more than any other. His sharp focus on it in the story makes his attitude limpid:

Aunt Rachel had gradually risen, while she warmed to her subject, and now she towered above us, black against the stars.

'Dey put chains on us an put us on a stan' as high as dis po'ch – twenty foot high – an all de people stood aroun', crowds and crowds. An' dey'd come up dah an look at us all roun', an squeeze our arm, and make us git up an walk, and den say, 'Dis one too ole,' or 'Dis one don't 'mount to much.' An dey sole my ole man, an took him away, and dey begin to sell my chil'en an take *dem* away, an I begin to cry; an de man say, 'Shet up yo' damn blubberin', an hit me on de mouf wid his han'. An when de las' one was gone but little Henry. I grab *him* clost up to my breas' so, an I ris up an says, 'You shan't take him away,' I says; 'I'll kill de man dat tetches him!' I

67

I think it is fair to characterise the novel in these passionate terms, in spite of our continuing argument that it was a carefully blueprinted undertaking. For all Twain's consciously recurring imagery and symbols, *Huckleberry Finn* consistently impresses one as a novel that has stumbled upon greatness. Twain's mode of literary creation, according to those who knew him, was to pour his personality on to the page, throwing each completed sheet in succession on the floor around him. At the end of the session he would collect up what he had written and have it typed. But he rarely planned his day's work, and would just keep going until inspiration failed. Then he would turn to something else.

Huckleberry Finn was, as we have seen, no exception. Written spasmodically over seven years, it was revised and retouched almost up to the moment of publication. It differed from Twain's other fiction in this respect, however, that it was written from the deepest sources of his boyhood experience. What marks this novel off, stylistically, from most of Twain's other work — I mean apart from Huck's rich exploitation of language, which we will consider more fully presently — is what we could call the accuracy of Twain's detailed eye. Most aspects of white Southern existence in the pre-war period come under his probing focus, and his recording is meticulous.[1] The power of his writing derives from the gradual but ultimately overwhelming accretion of striking and unforgetable detail.

Of course, this process is not genuinely or meaningfully

says. But my little Henry whisper an say, 'I gwyne to run away, an den work to buy yo' freedom.' Oh, bless de chile, he always so good! But dey got him — dey got him, de men did; but I took and tear de clo'es mos' off of 'em an beat em over de head wid my chain; an *dey* give it to me, too, but I didn't mine dat.'

(*Sketches New and Old*, New York, 1917, pp. 242-3.)

[1] This kind of point emphasises the importance of an historical perspective for literary critics — the obverse of the case for considering literature as historical evidence. A full response to any literary work must include situating it in time and place. An illustration from *Huckleberry Finn* may clinch the matter. Twain has frequently been attacked for making Jim improbably flee South, when liberty lay easily to the West or North. But as the historian Richard Wade points out, in *Slavery and the Cities* (New York, 1964), escaping slaves often took a Southern route to the large cities, where they were able to find work and anonymity. Twain, writing at first hand, was a better historian than his critics realise.

separable from Twain's linguistic inventiveness. All other considerations aside, *Huckleberry Finn* would be an epoch-making book for this one reason alone — Twain's striking creation of literary Amerenglish. Above all it is the stress and flux of the novel's sentences, and the evocative power of its extraordinary vocabulary, which leaves the reader with his sense of having been along the river with Huck Finn. The tensile strength in the following passage, for example, which displays Twain's inventiveness at its best, derives as much from para-neologisms as 'spider-webby' and 'blue-black' as the build-up assault on our imaginative senses. Twain's prose here, in its cumulative intensity, is a microcosmic expression of his success in the novel as a whole:

Directly it began to rain, and it rained like all fury, too, and I never see the wind blow so. It was one of these regular summer storms. It would get so dark that it looked all blue-black outside, and lovely; and the rain would thrash along by so thick that the trees off a little ways looked dim and spider-webby; and here would come a blast of wind that would bend the trees down and turn up the pale underside of the leaves; and then a perfect ripper of a gust would follow along and set the branches to tossing their arms as if they was just wild; and next, when it was just about the bluest and blackest — *fst*! it was as bright as glory and you'd have a little glimpse of tree-tops a-plunging about, away off yonder in the storm, hundreds of yards further than you could see before; dark as sin again in a second, and now you'd hear the thunder let go with an awful crash and then go rumbling, grumbling, tumbling down the sky towards the under side of the world, like rolling empty barrels down stairs, where it's long stairs and they bounce a good deal, you know.

(*Huckleberry Finn*, Chapter 9.)

This celebrated passage is so graphic that one realises with surprise that its decisive sentence, stylistically speaking, is also its

[1] A major ommission is, of course, sexuality. Those critics who attack both Twain and *Huck* for their failure to confront what would have been a major preoccupation in the case of an adolescent boy, seem to me unquestionably right. Nevertheless it strikes one as idle to demand that Twain ought to have written another novel, or to overlook the obvious limitations of Victorian social convention. Huck is simply not Holden Caulfield, whatever their other affinities.

most banal and prosaic: 'It was one of these regular summer storms.' The approach to what is typical and representative, in this case as elsewhere in the novel, is what releases Twain from the oppression of self-conscious poetry — Victorian prettiness — allowing him to indulge his descriptive powers to the full without appearing to strain for dramatic effect. Yet it is a highly theatrical, one might almost say Gothic, passage, full of vivid effects made up by the accumulation of a series of painterly details: the dark sky and driving rain, the pale undersides of the leaves flashing in the lightning, and the rolling thunder disappearing below the horizon. Twain creates an almost hypnotic mood in just a few sentences, and then snaps us out of it gently with Huck's disingenuous 'you know'. We're back in the world of boyhood adventure, where bouncing barrels down the stairs of empty houses is mischievous fun because they smash and make a glorious noise.

But beyond these obvious strengths it is Huck's regional accent that makes this passage, and indeed the rest of the novel, so aurally memorable. He writes with a noticable drawl. Twain was of course perfectly aware of it, delighting in his discovery that the language of his boyhood, its rich, colloquial looseness, might be turned into literary art. (As a public speaker in later years he was said to exaggerate his own speech pattern for the same reason.) And more: he was explicitly proud of the fact that, in his judgment, he had captured the authentic note of the American provinces. In a short preface he tells the reader to expect at least six shades 'of the backwoods South-Western dialect', adding: 'The shadings have not been done in any hap-hazard fashion, or by guess-work; but pains-takingly, and with the trustworthy guidance and support of personal familiarity with these several forms of speech.'

In point of fact, as we noted earlier regarding Black language, Twain was not always completely successful in this endeavour. The rather self-conscious eye-dialect renderings of working-class speech in the 'loafers' passage is another instance. But Huck's voice rings unmistakably true, because of course it was Twain's own. He wrote as he spoke. Consequently the flow of grammar and vocabulary are so wholly natural and so confidently done, that Huck is able to induct us into his linguistic universe within a few lines:

> You don't know about me, without you have read a book
> by the name of *The Adventures of Tom Sawyer*, but that ain't

70

no matter. That book was made by Mr Mark Twain, and he
told the truth, mainly. There was things which he stretched,
but mainly he told the truth. That is nothing. I never seen anybody but lied, one time or another, without it was Aunt Polly,
or the widow, or maybe Mary. Aunt Polly — Tom's Aunt Polly
she is — and Mary, and the Widow Douglas, is all told about
in that book — which is mostly a true book; with some stretchers, as I said before.

(Huckleberry Finn, Chapter 1.)

Twain involves us in Huck's circumstances so quickly (who is
Aunt Polly? Mary? The dishonest Mr Mark Twain, etc.?) that we
don't notice our more or less rapid entanglement in his vocabulary
and speech rhythms. Yet by the end of the first paragraph we
have already acquired a sense of Huck's repetitive lilt (a characteristic instance is the final sentence in the quotation) and have
learned that the past tense of 'see' is 'seen', and that 'without' can
also mean 'excepting'. Our sense of English has already shifted
and we are, linguistically speaking, off-balance and expectant.
The process is so unobtrusively compelling that we soon accept
the language conventions which later permit Huck's extraordinary
grammatical transformations, in the Chomskyan sense, to sound
perfectly natural and even logical. For example, when he disguises
himself as a little girl and calls on Mrs Judith Loftus, he tells us
how 'she got to talking about her husband, and about her relations
up the river, and about how much better off they used to was. . .'
(Chapter 11). Extrapolated from the text it looks like a misprint;
but in context it is barely noticeable. We have been taught to
speak Finnian.

Elsewhere Huck plays havoc with past tenses, spawning adverbs,
adjectives and verbs themselves with the neological abandon of a
man inventing a whole new language. There is the 'cluttering' of
bullfrogs on the river before dawn (Chapter 19), and the 'screaking'
of a sweep in its lock as a raft is rowed by (Chapter 19). Frightened people 'skaddle' out of the reach of danger (Chapter 22), girls
'brisken' up a room, and when you steal something you 'smouch'
it. In one of the novel's great scenes, the Wilks funeral (Chapter
27), an undertaker is described as having 'softy soothering ways',
while a 'melodeum' at the back of the room sounds 'pretty
skreeky' and colicky. The past tense of 'climb' is given, much

71

more strongly, as 'clumb' and Jim, in his story about his deaf daughter, 'crope' instead of 'crept' towards her (Chapter 23).

Twain's inventiveness is almost unlimited, verging on a kind of poetry. One of the strengths of the passage describing the storm, for instance, is the sheer beauty of the language. Elsewhere Tom Sawyer, Huck tells us, is not the sort of boy to 'meeky' along in a timid fashion, while in yet another fine characterisation of the wind he speaks of the way it 'swished and swushed' by. As this example illustrates, Twain had deep sense of the onomatopoeic. Later he employs it to invent the vowel-less verb:

> Blamed if the king didn't have to brace up mighty quick, or he'd a squshed down like a bluff bank that the river has cut under, it took him so sudden — and mind you, it was a thing that was calculated to make most *anybody* sqush...
>
> (*Huckleberry Finn*, Chapter 29.)

Inventions like these enable him to import a kind of infectious irresponsibility into his prose, so that he can communicate things beyond the surface meanings of words themselves. Mrs Loftus's little solecism, for example, (how much better off they used to was), adds a further dimension to what we subsequently learn about the experience of poverty in the deep South at that time. The actual language of the poor tells us something about poverty itself. On a lighter note Twain is able to say things like this:

> The duke, he never let on he suspicioned what was up, but just went goo-gooing around, happy and satisfied, like a jug that's googling out buttermilk...
>
> (*Huckleberry Finn*, Chapter 29.)

The humour, the vividness and the very Americanness of this moment are inseparable from Huck's capacity to make a past-tense verb out of 'suspicion' and to invent the outrageous simile that hinges on the non-existent participle, 'googling'. Its effectiveness, however, is undeniable.

The point is, of course, that Twain was not merely writing prose. He was recording the speech of a way of life. *Huckleberry Finn* is one of the most aural novels in the language, and in order for it to be so Twain had to depart from the polite cadences of educated grammar and take us into the sensuous unexpectedness of living words and forms. One has only to compare the stilted formality of the passage from *Tom Sawyer* given below with almost any example from *Huckleberry Finn* — for instance, the point at which Twain makes an intransitive verb out of 'dark' — 'the sky was darking up' — and speaks of the lightning beginning to 'wink and flitter' — to be aware of the enormous narrative advance that has been achieved. Twain's success is to striking that Huck is finally able to make us co-conspirators in his subversion of our language. At one point he produces a memorable image of Mississippi night, glittering with the visual and tactile: 'Everything was dead quiet, and it looked late and *smelt* late.' And then, confident that he has us spell-bound: 'You know what I mean — I don't know the words to put it in.' It is the helpless resignation of a victor.

Twain's language in *Huckleberry Finn* is his most significant contribution to literature, comparable, in its of course considerably more modest way, to Chaucer's use of spoken English in *The Canterbury Tales* or Dante's use of Italian in the *Divina Commedia*. T.S. Eliot declared that Twain had 'purified the language of the tribe', and compared him in this respect with Swift and Dryden. He was 'one of those writers, of whom there are not a great many in literature, who have discovered a new way of writing, valid not only for themselves but for others.' ('American Literature and the American Language,' *Washington University Studies*, No. 23, St Louis, 1953, pp. 16-17.)

Twain's linguistic inventiveness apart, however, his commitment to what I earlier called the representative and the typical, in other words, to the truth of a given situation, is the major stylistic mode in *Huckleberry Finn*. The two innovations combine to make it the most important novel written in nineteenth century America. Moreover, as a literary device Twain's recourse to the aural and observable fact is not found elsewhere in his fiction in such consistent application, though of course it is the greatest strength of his travel books and other non-fiction studies. *Huckleberry Finn* thus anticipated what was to become a major characteristic of writing in the next century — the increased blurring of the distinction between documentary and fiction. In a wholly valid and legitimate way Twain's novel can be considered almost a dramatised casebook, a living study in geographic, political and sociological actuality which, when taken together, yield a supremely fine work of literary art.

These points can best be illustrated by taking a close look at Twain's treatment of Southern racism and slavery. And the arch-racist in the novel is Pap Finn. He is a real white man.

> He was most fifty, and he looked it. His hair was long and tangled and greasy, and hung down, and you could see his eyes shining through like he was behind vines. It was all black, no gray; so was his long, mixed-up whiskers. There warn't no color in his face, where his face showed: it was white; not like another man's white, but a white to make a body sick, a white to make a body's flesh crawl — a tree-toad white, a fish-belly white.
>
> (*Huckleberry Finn*, Chapter 5.)

He is like a middle-aged version of Peter Verkhovensky, sinister and repellent in his pale ugliness: 'He looked a little ill, but it only seemed so. He had wrinkles on each cheek and near his cheekbones, which made him look like a man who had just recovered from a serious illness. And yet he was perfectly well and strong, and he had never been ill.' (Dostoevsky, *The Possessed*, Penguin, 1969, p. 187.)

Twain and Dostoevsky make us shudder, and for similar reasons. These are their villains, and nothing disgusted the Victorians quite so much as unhealthy-looking flesh. Pap is the reincarnation of Injun Joe, come again to steal Huck's cash and slit his throat.

But unlike Peter Verkovensky, Pap was drawn from life. He was based, as Twain indicated in his *Autobiography*, on Jimmy Finn, Hannibal's town drunkard. More than this, however, his sickly whiteness, emphasised by the black greasiness of his locks, relates organically to the value-structure of the novel. (In *The Possessed* Peter's anaemic glance has nothing to do with his politics.) Pap is the first, and in many ways the most viciously articulate, exponent of Southern racism. So his whiteness, as to a certain extent Moby Dick's, acts on both the literal and symbolic levels — he is simultaneously a white man and The White Man; a living emblem of European prejudice against Blacks and its most vivid embodiment. And at the same time, of course, because of all these things *and* because he is so physically revolting, he is meant to fill us with loathing. (Dostoevsky attempts the same inferential equation in *The Possessed*, but fails because he has to caricature Peter Verkhovensky's attitudes. No serious revolutionist ever

speaks with such gratuitously malign hysteria.[1] B
case, I will argue, Twain if anything understates the ma

Pap, the typical and representative Southern poo
also the archetypal Southern racist. Twain was aware th
often went together, as we will see. His eloquent
situated early in the novel, release into the narrative atmosphere
a kind of racist miasma that makes Jim's flight credible and adds
significance to many of the pivotal encounters in the action, such
as the coming of the bounty hunters and the recapture by the
Phelpses. From Pap we learn not only that there are free Blacks
as well as bondsmen in the South and that many are educated
far beyond his comprehension or capacity, but that the perni-
cious Southern slave system puts such people dangerously within
the power of such barbarians as Pap himself:

> 'Oh, yes, this is a wonderful govment, wonderful. Why,
> looky here. There was a free nigger there, from Ohio. A mul-
> atter, most as white as a white man. He had the whitest shirt
> on you ever see, too, and the shiniest hat; and there ain't a
> man in that town that's got as fine clothes as what he had;
> and he had a gold watch and chain, and a silver-headed cane —
> the awfulest old gray-headed nabob in the State. And what do
> you think? they said he was a p'fessor in a college, and could
> talk all kinds of languages, and knowed everything.'
>
> > (*Huckleberry Finn*, Chapter 6.)

Twain is pointing to the enormous, almost superhuman
ability of men like this anonymous professor who had not only
to overcome the enforced illiteracy of their people, but mastered
several languages and were able to teach them — to whites. Just
what this meant, in terms of sheer achievement, may have been
more apparent to Twain's contemporaries than it is to us. As
Kenneth Stampp points out, however, it was a cardinal precept of
slave law, in all the Southern states, that the skills of literacy
were forbidden Blacks. 'No person, not even the master, was to
teach a slave to read or write', or even 'employ him in setting
type in a printing office'. Needless to say it was also illegal to give
a slave books or pamphlets. (*The Peculiar Institution: Slavery in the
Ante-Bellum South,* Vintage Books, New York, 1956, p.208.)

---

[1] See Michael Egan and David Craig: 'Dostoevsky's Realism?' *Encounter*,
September 1973.

That some slaves thus actually learned to read, and then acquired several foreign languages and literatures, is a feat of staggering proportions. Because, as Genovese indicates, legislation merely codified existing social prejudices. Twain shows that he was aware of this too, when, after the evasion, he lets us watch the slaveholders and their wives wonder at the meaning of Jim's strange writings:

> 'Why, dog my cats, they must a ben a house-full o' niggers in there every night for four weeks, to a done all that work, Sister Phelps. Look at that shirt — every last inch of it kivered over with secret African writ'n done with blood! Must a ben a raft uv 'm at it right along, all the time, amost. Why, I'd give two dollars to have it read to me; 'n' as for the niggers that wrote it, I 'low I'd take 'n' lash'm t'll — —'
>
> (*Huckleberry Finn*, Chapter 41.)

Like Pap, Brother Marples would take and lash a nigger for writing. And more, for having written something he couldn't understand. The aggressive illiteracy of the speaker himself of course is also part of Twain's point, just as it is in the passage with Pap. These racist whites, Twain implies, are intellectually and humanly inferior to the blacks over whom they exercise the power of life and death. Under those circumstances it is a matter of wonder that, according to the estimate of Dr W.E. Burghardt Dubois, as much as five per cent of the slave population, that is about 200,000 people, possessed rudimentary literacy by 1860.

Twain seizes the opportunity of Pap's speech about the p'fessor to tell us something more about Southern anti-intellectualism, and the crushingly humiliating circumstances in which even a freed slave might find himself. That p'fessor, says Pap, taught in a college, and knew several languages and everything. But 'that ain't the wust.'

> 'They said he could *vote*, when he was at home. Well, that let me out. Thinks I, what is the country a-coming to? It was 'lection day, and I was just about to go and vote, myself, if I warn't too drunk to get there; but when they told me there was a State in this country where they'd let that nigger vote, I drawed out. I says I'll never vote agin. Them's the very words I said; and they all heard me; and the country may rot

76

for all me — I'll never vote agin as long as I live. And to see the
cool way of that nigger — why, he wouldn't give me the road if
I hadn't shoved him out o' the way. I says to the people, why
ain't this nigger put up at auction and sold? — that's what I
want to know. And what do you reckon they said? Why, they
said he couldn't be sold till he'd been in the State six months,
and he hadn't been there that long yet. There now — that's a
specimen. They call that govment that can't sell a free nigger
till he's been in the State six months. Here's a govment that
calls itself a govment, and yet's got to set stock-still for six
whole months before it can take ahold of a prowling, thieving,
infernal white-shirted free nigger, and —'

(Huckleberry Finn, Chapter 6.)

It is difficult to read this speech without mounting anger, because it's not funny. Pap condemns himself out of his own
mouth, of course, but these are the authentic tones of the
racist mentality. Pap would deny the vote to an educated
black, but won't exercise it himself or, when he does, is too
drunk to do so responsibly. Moreover, as he makes clear, any
white can shove any black out of his road with impunity. There
were many acts, said a North Carolina judge, which might constitute the legally punishable crime of 'insolence' by a black
man: it might merely be 'a look, the pointing of a finger, a
refusal or neglect to step out of the way when a white person
is seen to approach. But', he continued, 'each of such acts
violates the rules of propriety, and if tolerated, would destroy
that subordination upon which our social system rests.' (Quoted
in *The Peculiar Institution*, p.208.) What is more, as we can
gather from what Pap says, blacks were largely fair game for
whites. As Stampp confirms:

> Legally all white men were authorized to seize runaways; some
> of them, tempted by the rewards masters were willing to pay,
> made a profession out of it. Poor white men habitually kept
> their eyes open for strange Negroes without passes, for the
> apprehension of a fugitive was a financial windfall.

(The Peculiar Institution, p.153.)

This not only makes sense of Huck's and Jim's furtive flight —
they behave like conscripts in a beleaguered army behind the
enemy lines — but reveals the source and meaning of Pap's sour

77

viciousness. He shoves the black professor out of his road because that's all he can legally do. Habitually on the look-out for a quick buck by turning in a loose-running black he finds himself frustrated. (Like the king and the duke, who sell Jim for a quick $40, he is so alienated from his fellow man that he thinks nothing of trading another's liberty for a single poker session and a bottle of the local whiskey.)

Further, Pap will have felt paradoxically inferior to this particular Black whose social status so far exceeded his own. As Stampp remarks, 'slaves of all ranks ridiculed the non-slave-holders, especially the poor whites — the dregs of a stratified white society — whom they scornfully called "po' buckra" and "white trash".' (p. 338.) Possibly by pushing him out of his way Pap hoped to provoke even the smallest sign of hostility; this would have entitled him to strike the man dead on the spot. Not only was this legally sanctioned (Stampp, pp. 221-4) but, as one former slave, Frederick Douglas, recalled in his memoirs, it was a common white saying at this time that it was 'worth but half a cent to kill a nigger, and half a cent to bury him.' (*My Bondage and My Freedom*, New York, 1855, p.127.) Twain's evidence thus confirms at every point the analyses of the historians; and more, he gives flesh and meaning to their cold assertions. The situation of the black professor is precisely that which Fogel and Engerman (who, incidentally, reject literary evidence out of hand) glancingly put this way: 'For blacks during the ante-bellum era, then, freedom and slavery were not separated by a sharp dividing line. One gradually shaded into the other.' (*Time on the Cross:The Economics of Southern Slavery*, Little Brown & Co., Boston, 1974, p. 244.)

Pap, the typical white racist, is portrayed as a man corrupted and even destroyed by his society: he is, after all, one possible version of Huck grown up. In his maturity he has come to embody all the worst and characteristic features of his South: he is greedy, prejudiced and of course incorrigibly violent. Moreover, drink is his life — and death. (As Genovese shows, alcohol abuse was a distinct feature among Southern whites at this time: 'The use of whiskey in white homes of all classes caused visitors to gasp.' (*Roll, Jordan, Roll: The World the Slaves Made,* New York, 1974, p.645.) The temperance movement was also strong, as Pap discovers.) Thus one of the most distressing scenes in the novel, Pap's attack of *delirium tremens,*was included partly for what it said about the

78

whites and not merely for the sake of melodrama. He screams in terror, imagining there are snakes crawling all over him: 'I never see a man look so wild in the eyes...then he rolled over and over, wonderful fast, kicking things every which way, and striking and grabbing at the air with his hands, and screaming...' (Chapter 6.) It is like a scene from *The Lost Weekend*, though Twain was no abstentionist. What he is actually implying is: this is the face of white supremacy.

Twain was not, however, interested in merely pilloring the Paps of the prewar era. His real target was slavery itself, but in order to understand it — Twain suggests — it is necessary to know something about the racists themselves. And who better to communicate their authentic accents than a former Southern racist?

For Twain had been a typical product of his world until he travelled out of it. What he had to say about his mother in his *Autobiography* was true also of himself, as he well knew:

> As I have said, we lived in a slaveholding community; indeed, when slavery perished my mother had been in daily touch with it for sixty years. Yet, king-hearted and compassionate as she was, I think she was not conscious that slavery was a bald, grotesque and unwarrantable usurpation. She had never heard it assailed in any pulpit, but she heard it defended and sanctified in a thousand; her ears were familiar with Bible texts that approved it, but if there were any that disapproved it they had not been quoted by her pastors; as far as her experience went, the wise and the good and the holy were unanimous in the conviction that slavery was right, righteous, sacred, the peculiar pet of the Deity, and a condition which the slave himself ought to be daily and nightly thankful for. Manifestly, training and association can accomplish strange miracles...There was nothing about the slavery of the Hannibal region to rouse one's dozing humane instincts to activity.
>
> (*Mark Twain's Autobiography*, I, pp. 123-4.)

Under these circumstances it is hardly surprising that Twain adopted the prejudices of his boyhood world. After he went East in 1853 he wrote home several times expressing his amazement and disgust at the way Blacks were allowed to mix socially with whites: 'to wade through this mass of human vermin', he exclaimed in a letter to his mother, 'would raise the ire of the most patient person that ever lived.' And in another letter: 'I reckon I had better black my face, for in these Eastern States niggers are considerably better than white people.'

By the time he came to write *Huckleberry Finn*, however, Twain had of course rid himself of much of his early prejudice – though not entirely. Little racist tics continued to display themselves in his work – a small example, which we have already discussed, is the patronising way he refers to Uncle Dan'l, the respected and intelligent slave on his uncle John Quarles's plantation. 'He had an uncommon level head, for a nigger', declares Huck of Jim, thus revealing his racism. But this remark is not substantially different from Twain's own kindly estimate of Dan'l, who had much the best head on the plantation – in the negro quarter. As Genovese puts it, 'Every planter boasted of the physical or intellectual prowess of one or more of his blacks, much as the strictest father might boast of the prowess of a favoured child.' (*Roll, Jordan, Roll*, p.73.) Twain was still at it in 1898.

Nevertheless, he was able to be considerably objective about race prejudice, which is not the same as saying he was detached, and communicate his sense of its insidiousness. He understood clearly that the whole brutal oppression of slavery was underpinned by a set of mental habits which enabled whites to regard other human beings as in some way less than human. The passage about his mother I quoted earlier, for instance, continues a few lines later: 'I have no recollection of ever seeing a slave auction in that town; but I am suspicious that this is because the thing was a common and commonplace spectacle, not an uncommon and impressive one.' Twain realised that if blacks could be thought of as less than human they could of course be treated accordingly. Racism is thus literally dehumanising.

Naturally Huck is, like his father, a racist. What else would he be? The novel's structure of feeling, in Raymond Williams's vivid phrase, pivots on his growing comprehension that the racist 'truths' of his upbringing are a monstrous political perversion. At first, and indeed for most of the journey down river, he allows Jim to cook for him, care for him, sleep rougher and work longer hours. He thinks nothing of leaving his friend bound and gagged for hours on the raft while he and the king and the duke are ashore upon some escapade. After the fog sequence, when he and Jim are joyfully reunited, he cruelly mocks the black man's delight and makes a sport of his devotion. But the climax of this scene marks one of the moments in Huck's increasing understanding:

'What do they stan' for? I's gwyne tell you. When I got all wore out wid work, en wid de callin for you, en went to sleep, my heart wuz mos' broke bekase you wuz los', an I didn' k'yer no mo' what become er me en de raf'. En when I wake up en fine you back agin', all safe en soun', de tears come en I could a got down on my knees en kiss yo' foot I's so thankful. En all you wuz thinkin 'bout wuz how you could make a fool uv ole Jim wid a lie. Dat truck dah is *trash*; en trash is what people is dat puts on de head er dey fren's en makes em ashamed.'

Then he got up slow, and walked to the wigwam, and went in there, without saying anything but that. But that was enough. It made me feel so mean I could almost kissed *his* foot to get him to take it back.

It was fifteen minutes before I could work myself up to go and humble myself to a nigger – but I done it, and warn't ever sorry for it afterwards, neither. I didn't do him no more mean tricks, and I wouldn't done that one if I'd a knowed it would make him feel that way.

(*Huckleberry Finn*, Chapter 15.)

Twain was realist enough, and sufficiently unsentimental, not to pretend that Huck ever ceased to oppose blacks and whites in his mind as conventional images of evil and good. 'I knowed he was white inside', he thinks warmly of Jim towards the end of the novel – the highest praise he can bestow. The irony in the passage quoted above is that Huck still sees Jim as a menial, and considers himself enormously virtuous for having apologised, 'humbling' himself to a 'nigger'. In other words, Jim may have had more of the human about him than Huck at first realises, but this doesn't mean that he ever sees him or any other black as a real person. He's just a very intelligent animal. 'All right, trot ahead', he tells the black man ('my nigger') who has come to lead him to Jim at the end of the Grangerford sequence. At another point he exclaims in disgust: 'Well, if ever I struck anything like it I'm a nigger'.

Huck is also prone to think in the anaesthetising, cant phrases of institutionalised racism when confronting severe moral problems about Jim. 'Give a nigger an inch and he'll take an ell', he reminds

81

himself as he slowly resolve to betray him before he can get to
Cairo. And: 'Everybody naturally despises an ungrateful nigger',
– this, just before his final resolution to rescue Jim and go to Hell.
The closest Huck ever gets to the truth is his incredulous conclusion that Jim is really very human, that is, white:

> I went to sleep, and Jim didn't call me when it was my turn.
> He often done that. When I waked up, just at day-break, he was
> setting there with his head down betwixt his knees, moaning
> and mourning to himself. I didn't take notice, nor let on. I
> knowed what it was about. He was thinking about his wife and
> his children, away up yonder, and he was low and homesick;
> because he hadn't ever been away from home before in his life;
> and I do believe he cared just as much for his people as white
> folks does for their'n. It don't seem natural, but I reckon it's
> so. He was often moaning and mourning that way, nights, when
> he judged I was asleep, and saying, 'Po' little 'Lizabeth! po'
> little Johnny! it's mighty hard; I spec' I ain't gwyne to see you
> no mo', no mo'!' He was a mighty good nigger, Jim was.

> (*Huckleberry Finn*, Chapter 23.)

Huck never loses his sense of race identity. He is its victim.
Stampp puts it this way: 'Most white men were obsessed with the
terrible urgency of racial solidarity, with the fear that the whole
complex mechanism of control would break down if the master's
discretion in governing slaves were questioned.' (*The Peculiar
Institution*, p. 222.) In the greater finesse of Twain's novel this
becomes Huck's torment at the prospect of Jim's acquiring his
liberty: 'Thinks I, this is what comes of my not thinking. Here was
this nigger which I had as good as helped to run away, coming right
out flat-footed and saying he would steal his children – children
that belonged to a man I didn't even know; a man that hadn't
ever done me no harm.' The distorted values of the slave system,
and everything that propped it up, are dramatised in this
sequence as we realise that Huck seriously believes that Jim has
less right to his own children – poor little Elizabeth and poor little
Johnny – than the white owner who may have bought them
literally by the pound at a slave auction. Twain makes the same
point in similar words on the later occasion as well, when Huck
considers writing to Miss Watson. He thinks of himself as 'stealing
a poor old woman's nigger that hadn't ever done me on harm'

82

Again Twain uses the same linguistic ambiguity to remind the reader that Jim is harmless, and human, too; so he is able to characterise the mood while simultaneously implying a comment on it. This is his 'radical objectivity' in action.

Jim, of course, is a racist as well. He accepts without serious question the myth of his own genetic inferiority, and never challenges the right of whites to their property — including slaves. It is only when he is confronted by the prospect of forcible separation from his wife and children that he rebels. Even then his rebellion is negative; he refuses merely to be sold down river. In other words, Jim is no Nat Turner. After his flight and subsequent recapture he continues to perceive the world with the eyes and consciousness of a white racist. Like so many other runaways, as Genovese illustrates, he is overcome by a sense of guilt, and resolves to work for the liberty of his children and wife through the 'legal' channels first, before calling on the despised Abolitionists for assistance.

Twain is half-consciously demonstrating one of the ways social contempt theories operate. They induce the victim to participate in his or her own oppression through devices such as constant repetition and education, and by institutional, legislative and ideological reinforcement (such as religion) at all levels. Like Mark Twain himself, Jim has no alternative but to accept the unargued assumptions of his society so long as he remains a part of it.

Twain makes something of a joke of this, though the seriousness of his intent can be easily distinguished because it is never far below the surface. For example, Huck and Jim discuss France and the French language. Jim is asked: 'Spose a man was to come to you and say *Polly-voo-Franzy* — what would you think?' His reply is overtly a Twainian jest — the humour in this situation, after all, derives once more precisely from the tension between his double address to a twin but discreetly separated audience. Still, what Jim says is worth more than a giggle: 'I wouldn't think nuff'n; I'd take en bust him over the head. Dat is, if he warn't white. I wouldn't 'low no nigger to call me dat.' (Chapter 14.) In other words, niggers have to know their place. Even with other niggers. An insult from a white, however, is met with grovelling gratitude. Jim's world, like Huck's, comprises niggers and white men, respect and equality, deference and contempt. Jim knows, and accepts, the limits of both.

Moreover, his racism is shown to be typical and representative

83

of the Southern black. He recovers the raft, while Huck is at the Grangerfords, by demanding of the local slaves who found it whether 'dey gwyne to grab a young white genlman's propaty, en git a hid'n for it? Den I gin 'm ten cents apiece, en dey 'uz mighty well satisfied, en wisht some mo' raf's 'd come along and make 'm rich agin.' (Chapter 18.) The pathetic contrast between Jim's idea of wealth — fourteen dollars — and the actual riches present in this society has already been established by this point. So his cunning shows a further aspect of his developing social consciousness. He is learning the rules of the racist game from the white perspective, and finds he can turn them occasionally to his own advantage — against other blacks. Genovese quotes one white eye-witness, Fanny Kemble, supporting a similar point :

> The command of one slave to another is altogether the most uncompromising utterance of insolent, truculent despotism that it ever befell my lot to witness or listen to. 'You nigger — I say you black nigger — you no hear me call you — what for you no run quick?' . . . I assure you, no contemptuous white intonation ever equalled the *prepotenza* of the despotic insolence of this address of these poor wretches to each other.
>
> (*Roll, Jordan, Roll*, p. 380.)

Nevertheless, as Genovese makes clear elsewhere, racial solidarity among the blacks was as wide-spread as among the whites. 'The ways in which the slaves displayed solidarity often entailed considerable personal risk.' (p.623.) Again Twain supports the historian and gives life and flesh to his statements. We see the Grangerford slaves, for example, concealing Jim and feeding him from their own rations, and finally leading Huck back to him, although the penalties for assisting runaways were severe and violent, ranging from incarceration to whipping — up to the legal maximum of thirty-nine lashes — or both. Other common punishments included 'burning in the hand', and the barbarous ear-cropping. (Stampp, p.210 ff.)

*   *   *

Twain's attitude towards slavery itself was equally unequivocal. He despised racism, but he realised that it was the consequence rather than the origin of the chattel system. It was a symbiotic

84

adjunct, an ideological outgrowth that both fed slavery and fed on it. Racism spoke both for and to the slaveholders. Thus his implicit political exhortation was not the conventional liberal plea to recognise common brotherhood but the revolutionary demand that the system be physically smashed.

Twain's writings about slavery returned repeatedly to a particular scene from his boyhood in Hannibal. Though almost trivial in itself it expressed one of the greatest evils of the slave system, the disintegration and separation of black families:

> There was, however, one small incident of my boyhood days which touched this matter, and it must have meant a good deal to me or it would not have stayed in my memory, clear and sharp, vivid and shadowless, all these slow-drifting years. We had a little slave boy whom we had hired from someone, there in Hannibal. He was from the eastern shore of Maryland, and had been brought away from his family and his friends, halfway across the American continent, and sold. He was a cheery spirit, innocent and gentle, and the noisiest creature that ever was, perhaps. All day long he was singing, whistling, yelling, whooping, laughing — it was maddening, devastating, unendurable. At last, one day, I lost all my temper, and went raging to my mother and said Sandy had been singing for an hour without a single break, and I couldn't stand it, and *wouldn't* she please shut him up. The tears came to her eyes and her lip trembled, and she said something like this:
>
> 'Poor thing, when he sings it shows that he is not remembering, and that comforts me; but when he is still I am afraid he is thinking, and I cannot bear it. He will never see his mother again; if he can sing, I must not hinder it, but be thankful for it. If you were older you would understand me; then that friendless child's noice would make you glad.'
>
> It was a simple speech and made up of small words, but it went home, and Sandy's noise was not a trouble to me any more.

(*Mark Twain's Autobiography*, I, pp.101–2.)

The extent to which black families were broken up under auction has recently become something of an issue among historians. Fogel and Engerman have contended, on the basis of their statistical (econometric) analyses that the practice was far less

85

widespread than has previously been thought. Their argument is that the 'economic forces' that led the planter 'to destroy, rather than maintain' slave families were 'relatively infrequent' in occurrence; and that it has been abolitionist propaganda, calculated 'to arouse sentiment against the slave system' and 'accepted so uncritically by historians' which has led to this belief. (*Time on the Cross*, p.143.)

This suggestion, however, simply will not hold up under scrutiny. First, Fogel and Engerman specifically reject as untrustworthy precisely the kind of evidence that would contradict their assertion, namely first-hand accounts of eye-witnesses who were there. They say in their first chapter:

> We have least confidence in fragmentary evidence which is based on unverifiable impressions of individuals whose primary aim was the defense of an ideological position. Fragmentary evidence from objective sources, such as impressionistic reports of 'detached' observers may be more believable, but is still of a low order of reliability since it is usually not possible to submit such evidence to systematic statistical tests. . . Arguments that rest on impressionistic, fragmentary evidence must be considered to be on a relatively low level of reliability, regardless of the objectivity of the source of this evidence.
>
> (*Time on the Cross*, pp.10–11.)

As Genovese points out, however, the data in this kind of case not being available, 'do not permit precise measurement', (*Roll, Jordan, Roll,* p.457.) It is exactly under these circumstances that we have to turn to those whom the cliometricians refuse to consult, that is, those who were there. The son of one planter, quoted by Genovese, was for instance quite unequivocal when the question was put to him. " 'Were families separated by sale, etc?" 'Yes, quite often'. " Reluctance to face up to this kind of testimony is not only damning in historians but, in the case of *Time on The Cross* actually brings out a truth about the book that commentators have been reluctant to admit: namely, that it is, whatever the pious protestations of its authors, actually an apology for chattel slavery. Consequently its authors have sought to minimise the barbarous features of the system at every point, suggesting even that in a substantial number of cases 'whipping was as mildly applied as the corporal punishment normally practised within families today.'

(p.145.) An honest man might answer that, first, it is not possible to whip anyone 'mildly', even once, and secondly, that the physical chastisement of children, even severely done, cannot 'normally' be compared – under any circumstances – to a last of the whip.

There is a second and more forceful rebuttal of *Time on the Cross*, however, and that is the evidence contained in literature. We have seen and will see repeatedly in the present study that, first, literature and even so-called fiction can indeed be excellent evidence and, moreover, that it can provide insights and details precisely unavailable to the conventional historian. Furthermore, we have repeatedly shown the way in which Twain in *Huckleberry Finn* sought to be typical and representative in the images of society he brought to his readers. In each instance Twain's testimony has stood up, both against the academic histories and against the test of literary analysis – the argument being that if the writing failed to be of the first rank it was likely that the evidence it contained was also untrustworthy.

On the issue of callously disintegrated families Twain's evidence soundly contradicts the cliometricians. The plot of the entire book, for example, revolves around the threat of Jim's being sold down the river, away from his family. We have already discussed his lamentation over his children. Miss Watson's decision to sell him away, moreover, is of the most inhumane and calculating sort. What happened was, first, that after Tom Sawyer's silly trick on Jim, which leaves the black man believing that something supernatural has occurred, 'Jim was most ruined, for a servant, because he got so stuck up on account of having seen the devil and been rode by witches.' (Chapter 2.) Thus, when the slave trader comes sniffing around Miss Watson's establishment, offering her a good price for Jim, she resolves to sell him down the river. Jim tells Huck:

'Well, you, it 'uz dis way. Ole Missus – dat's Miss Watson – she pecks on me all de time, en treats me pooty rough, but she awluz said she wouldn' sell me down to Orleans. But I noticed dey was a nigger trader roun' de place considable, lately, en I begin to git oneasy. Well, one night I creeps to de do', pooty late, en de do' warn't quite shet, en I hear ole missus tell de widder she gwyne to sell me down to Orleans, but she didn' want to, but she could git eight hund'd dollars for me, en it

'uz sich a big stack o money she couldn' resis'. De widder she
try to git her to say she wouldn' do it, but I never waited to
hear de res'. I lit out mighty quick, I tell you.'

(*Huckleberry Finn*, Chapter 8.)

Twain shows that whites were not without humane considerations, but that economic and legal factors invariably outweighed
them when the issue came to the test. Miss Watson is actually
planning the most treacherous betrayal open to her — breaking
her repeatedly-given word, secreatly concluding a deal with the
trader, reconciling herself not only to Jim's misery but to the fact
that she will be splintering his family (he has a wife and two
children) into irrevocable fragments. The Widow Douglas understands these things but never of course questions Miss Watson's
legal right to dispose of her chattel in any way she pleases. Jim
himself appreciates that eight hundred dollars is a lot of money.

Jim's case, however, is by no means the only illustration of
criminally broken families in the novel. The king and the duke,
in their aliases as Peter Wilks's English cousins, quickly set about
disposing of his property, including his slaves.

So the next day after the funeral, along about noontime,
the girls' joy got the first jolt; a couple of nigger traders come
along.[1] and the king sold them the niggers reasonable, for three-
day drafts as they called it, and away they went, the two sons
up the river to Memphis, and their mother down the river to
Orleans. I thought them poor girls and them niggers would
break their hearts for grief; they cried round each other, and
took on so it most made me down sick to see it. The girls
said they hadn't ever dreamed of seeing the family separated

---

[1] At least one commentator chides Twain for the hollow coincidence of
this arrival. However as Stampp confirms, 'Most of the traders operated on
a small scale with limited capital. In the exporting states they attended
estate and execution sales and sought out private owners who wished to dispose of a slave or two. After purchasing a few dozen slaves they organised
them into a coffle and drove them southward to the cotton and sugar
districts'. (*The Peculiar Institution*, p.260.) Huck's confidence at the end
of the passage that these slaves would eventually be returned appears also
to have some basis in fact. Stampp remarks: 'There were virtually no
restrictions upon the owner's right to deed his bondsmen to others. Normally the courts nullified such transfers only if the seller fraudulently
warranted a slave to be "free from defects" or vices such as the "habit of
running away." ' (p.199.)

or sold away from the town. I can't ever get it out of my memory, the sight of them poor miserable girls and niggers hanging around each other's necks and crying; and I reckoned I couldn't a stood it at all but would a had to bust out and tell on our gang if I hadn't knowed the sale warn't no account and the niggers would be back home in a week or two.

(*Huckleberry Finn*, Chapter 27.)

This could hardly be characterised as abolitionist propaganda. Indeed what marks it is the way Twain steers as far as he can from rhetoric and melodrama while remaining close to the facts of the scene. And he is obviously describing something all too familiar. His scrupulousness as an observer makes itself apparent at every juncture, from the realised specificity of 'three-day drafts' and the exact destinations of the slaves, to the shocked dismay of the actual owners who feel closely attached to their servants of many years' standing. Twain shows that he knew perfectly well that close ties of affection bound master and slave in the South just as strongly as animosities and hatreds pushed them apart.

Twain also makes it clear that, as both Genovese and Stampp record, whites were often extremely reluctant to break up slave families. Stampp especially notes that, just as Twain's scene dramatises, separations nevertheless occurred particularly following the slaveholder's death. In other words, Twain remains true to his commitment to deal with the representative and typical. Stampp moreover makes the point that the dispersal of slave families tended to occur when, precisely as in Peter Wilks's case, the master died intestate. He comments:

In such cases the southern courts seldom tried to prevent the breaking up of slave families. The executor of an estate was expected to dispose of human chattels, like other property, in the way that was most profitable to the heirs. It may be 'harsh' to separate members of families, said the North Carolina Supreme Court, yet 'it must be done, if the executor discovers that the interest of the estate requires it; for he is not to indulge his charities at the expense of others.'

(*The Peculiar Institution*, p.199.)

This is exactly the attitude among the townspeople in Twain's story. They are angered by the king's action but do not challenge its legality or necessity. 'The thing made a big stir in the town, too', Huck comments, 'and a good many come out flat-footed and said it was scandalous to separate the mother and children that way.' In other words, Twain was a good enough witness not only correctly to judge the temper of the South but was also honest enough to let us know that attitudes towards Blacks covered a full repertoire of possibilities, from the grasping, cynical inhumanity of the king to the resentful mutterings among the townsfolk. What he also rightly shows is that not a soul, not even the compassionate Huck, reflects for a moment that the whole ghastly system might be at fault.

In *A Connecticut Yankee*, his next novel, Twain was more explicitly hostile to slavery. 'The blunting effects of slavery upon the slaveholder's moral perceptions are known and conceded, the world over', Hank remarks at one point; 'The repulsive feature of slavery is the thing, not its name.' And, in case the reader has missed the implicit target of his attack he says later, when he and King Arthur are being put up for auction as chattels:

> This same infernal law had existed in our own South in my own time, more than thirteen hundred years later, and under it hundreds of freemen who could not prove that they were free-men had been sold into life-long slavery without the circumstance making any particular impression upon me; but the minute law and the auction block came into my personal experience, a thing which had been merely improper before became suddenly hellish. Well, that's the way we are made.

> (*A Connecticut Yankee in King Arthur's Court*, Chapter 34.)

This comment glances reflexively back at the situation of the black professor so despised by Pap Finn; a man who, in spite of his paper freedom, might well be taken by force by such as Pap and sold into slavery down New Orleans way. Twain, however, keeps his steady focus on the issue that seems to have stirred him most deeply about the chattel system, the barbarity of splitting husbands, wives and children for a short-run economic gain. He is offended by the *powerlessness* of ordinary human beings to order their own fates. The tale 'A True Story' contains his most harrowing image of this helplessness; but *A Connecticut Yankee* is his most sustained. It is also, in the context we have established, his most remorseless indictment of the Southern system. The details he includes come clearly from affecting personal experiences:

> All these faces were gray with a coating of dust. One has seen the like of this coating upon furniture in unoccupied houses, and has written his idle thought in it with his finger. I was reminded of this when I noticed the faces of some of those women, young mothers carrying babes that were near to death and freedom, how a something in their hearts was written in the dust upon their faces, plain to see, and lord, how plain to read! for it was the track of tears.
>
> (*A Connecticut Yankee in King Arthur's Court*, Chapter 21.)

Hank and the King have come upon a coffle of British slaves. They are chained together, neck to ankle, 'bundled together like swine'. Their clothes are rags and tatters and they are driven forward by a slave trader armed with a whip. It is of course a familiar Southern scene; there were no slaves in sixth century Britain. Hank and his companions look on as one of the young women is lashed and 'a flake of skin from her naked shoulder' is flicked into the air. It is the kind of detail only an eyewitness would have dared to include. Twain's confidence with the scene extends to the on-lookers, who are unmoved by what they see. 'They were too much hardened by lifelong familiarty with slavery to notice that there was anything else in the exhibition that invited comment' — other than appreciating the slave trader's dexterity with the whip. 'This was what slavery could do, in the way of ossifying what one may call the superior lobe of human feeling; for these pilgrims were kind-hearted people and they would not have allowed that man to treat a horse like that.' (Chapter 21.)

They are of course Southern whites; more, they are, in a collective sense, Twain's own mother, the original (as Twain noted in his autobiography) of Aunts Polly and Sally. She, who tolerated slavery because she had never heard it opposed in any pulpit, one day in St Louis pulled the whip from the hand of 'a burly cartman who was beating his horse over the head with the butt' (*Autobiography*, I, pp.118—19). Still, like her countrymen, she saw nothing wrong with slavery, and Twain comments on the paradox in terms which explicitly recall the passage from *A Connecticut Yankee* just cited:

It is commonly believed that an infallible effect of slavery was to make such as lived in its midst hard-hearted. I think it had no such effect — speaking in general terms. I think it stupified everybody's humanity, as regarded the slave, but stopped there. There were no hard-hearted people in our town — I mean there were no more than would be found in any other town of the same size in any other country; and in my experience hard-hearted people are very rare everywhere.

(*Mark Twain's Autobiography*, I, p.125.)

It is this moral obtuseness, this same dulled familiarity with human misery, which enabled the pilgrims in *A Connecticut Yankee*, and the majority of whites in Twain's Hannibal, to gaze on unmoved as the greatest of all inhumanities was perpetrated, the physical separation of a loving family by the auctioneer:

Just here was the wayside shop of a smith; and now arrived a landed proprietor who had bought this girl a few miles back, deliverable here where her irons could be taken off. They were removed; then there was a squabble between the gentleman and the dealer as to which should pay the black-smith. The moment the girl was delivered from her irons, she flung herself, all tears and frantic sobbings, into the arms of the slave who had turned his face when she was whipped. He strained her to his breast, and smothered her face and the child's with kisses, and washed them with the rain of his tears. I suspected. I inquired. Yes, I was right; it was husband and wife. They had to be torn apart by force; the girl had to be dragged away, and she struggled and fought and shrieked like one gone mad till a turn of the road hid her from sight; and even after that, we could still make out the fading plaint of those receding shrieks. And the husband and father, with his wife and child gone, never to be seen by him again in life? — well, the look of him one might not bear at all, and so I turned away; but I knew I should never get his picture out of my mind again, and there it is to this day, to wring my heart-strings whenever I think of it.

(*A Connecticut Yankee in King Arthur's Court*, Chapter 21.)

Again, what distinguishes Twain's writing is that he manages to do justice to the scene without false emotionalism, without

92

bluster or deliberate tear-jerking. It is not an episode to weep over but one with which to share the author's evident anger. Like Huck in similar circumstances he is moved to the edge of protest rather than despair; and he carries us with him. Twain is inciting his readers to the barricades.

Elsewhere in the novel he makes a powerful plea for the class unity of all the Southern oppressed, black and white. His words in this context are obviously addressed to his white compatriots down South; but his main target is Pap Finn. Pap simply will not understand that his degradation rests, as surely as does Jim's, upon the chattel system itself. He will not see, as Twain came to see, that the poor everywhere need only unite to throw off the tyranny of their conditions and circumstances. And Pap does not understand finally, that it his own racism, induced by the corrupt economics of his world, that actually props up all the exploitation in St Petersburg:

> This was depressing — to a man with the dream of a republic in his head. It reminded me of a time thirteen centuries away, when the 'poor whites' of our South who were always despised and frequently insulted by the slave-lords around them, and who owed their base condition simply to the presence of slavery in their midst, were yet pusillanimously ready to side with the slave-lords in all political moves for the upholding and perpetuating of slavery, and did also finally shoulder their muskets and pour out their lives in an effort to prevent the destruction of that very institution which degraded them.
>
> (*A Connecticut Yankee in King Arthur's Court*, Chapter 30.)

Twain himself of course had been one of them, both in his poverty and in his willingness to fight for the Confederacy. Thus he also knew that this charcoal burner, who was 'just the twin of the Southern "poor white" of the far future' carried the elements of class struggle in his own heart nevertheless. Twain completes his passage, then, with another stirring call:

> And there was only one redeeming feature connected with that pitiful piece of history; and that was, that secretly the 'poor white' did detest the slave-lord, and did feel his own shame. That feeling was not brought to the surface, but the

fact that it was there and could have been brought out, under favouring circumstances, was something — in fact, it was enough; for it showed that a man is at bottom a man, after all, even if it doesn't show on the outside.

(*A Connecticut Yankee in King Arthur's Court*, Chapter 30.)

Twain's steely conviction is like Solzhenitsyn's, another writer uncompromisingly opposed to the oppression in his native land: 'We cannot accept that the murderous course of history is irremediable and that the human spirit that believes in itself cannot influence the most powerful force in the world. The experience of recent generations convinces me that only the unbending human spirit taking its stand on the front line against the violence that threatens it, ready to sacrifice itself and to die proclaiming "*Not one step further*" — only this inflexibility of the spirit can be the real defender of personal peace, and of all humanity.' (*New York Review of Books*, 4 October 1973.) Not only Boggs and Pap Finn, but all oppressed people, hover around the edges of Twain's lines.

We shall see how the rich specificity of Twain's fictional mode extended to such apparently irrelevant minutiae as the cash value of local products and social services. The effect of this is to add to Huck's narrative authority by increasing the palpability of his tale. The most telling figures, however, we can discuss immediately. These are the ones relating to chattel slavery itself.

Twain's close analysis bears out the subsequent judgements of the historians. On the basis of *Huckleberry Finn* we would correctly see that enslaved blacks were, apart from land, the most valuable commodities in the Southern economy. ('Commodity' is probably the right word to use here, since there were whole regions of the U.S.A. specialising in the breeding and exporting of saleable bodies for the sugar and cotton-growing plantations in the deeper South. That is, they were engaged in slave production and marketing, in producing slaves as commodities. (Cf. K. Marx, *Capital*, I, 41—97.).) Moreover, as Twain makes abundantly clear, blacks had both exchange and labour value and, in addition, were highly perishable. They were the ideal product.

Twain demonstrates that every aspect of the chattel system, even its impending collapse, carried the possibilities of profit for

94

someone – provided he or she were white. We learn that the reward on a runaway, for instance, varied between $200 and $300 – a substantial figure. The bounty hunters we hear about in chapter eleven, and actually encounter in chapter sixteen, were thus more than gainfully employed. Catch one fugitive and you net more than a steamboat pilot earns in half a year. Round up an entire batch and you can retire. So the sinister eagerness of the hunters, together with their evident affluence – each presses a $20 gold coin into Huck's hand when he persuades them that his family are suffering from small pox – has both point and irony. Stampp supports the tenor of Twain's scene and his statistics, citing a Mississippi farmer who employed a professional slave catcher: 'He follows a negro with his dogs 36 hours after he has passed and never fails to overtake him. It is his profession and he makes some $600 per annum by it.' (*The Peculiar Institution*, p.189.)

Once recovered a recalcitrant black was evidently worth a small cash fortune to his owner. Sold down the river, that is, to the cotton and sugar planters, he could fetch as much as $800 – no little amount to a householder like Miss Watson. And a good slave, which means what Fogel and Engerman call a 'prime' worker, that is, a strong male in his twenties, could be worth as much as $1,000 with 'good treatment' – no beating, better quality food, and so forth.

These figures establish a context, and therefore a meaning, for Twain's emphasis on the way cash values dominate human relations in the novel. I am thinking not only of the way money is used to bale out uneasy consciences, as the slave hunters do when they pay Huck and his supposed family to go away somewhere else and die, but the way that Pap suddenly rediscovers his paternal responsibilities when he hears that Huck has come into some money. Even more strikingly perhaps, one thinks of the way Judge Thatcher cheats Huck out of this same fortune:

'Why, my boy, you are all out of breath. Did you come for your interest?'

'No sir,' I says; 'is there some for me?'

'Oh, yes, a half-yearly, in last night. Over a hundred and fifty dollars. Quite a fortune for you. You better let me invest it along with your six thousand, because if you take it you'll spend it.'

'No sir,' I says, 'I don't want to spend it. I don't want it at all — nor the six thousand, nuther. I want you to take it; I want to give it to you — the six thousand and all.'

He looked surprised. He couldn't seem to make it out. He says:

'Why, what can you mean, my boy?'

I says, 'Don't you ask me no questions about it, please. You'll take it — won't you?'

He says:

'Well, I'm puzzled. Is something the matter?'

'Please take it,' says I, 'and don't ask me nothing — then I won't have to tell no lies.'

He studied a while, and then he says:

'Oho-o. I think I see. You want to *sell* all your property to me — not give it. That's the correct idea.'

Then he wrote something on a paper and read it over, and says:

'There — you see it says "for a consideration". That means I have bought it off you and paid you for it. Here's a dollar for you. Now, you sign it.'

So I signed it, and left.

(*Huckleberry Finn*, Chapter 4.)

The judge thus buys himself $6,000 for $1. Moreover, he never returns it. On the novel's penultimate page Tom briefly refers to the sum : ' "it's all there, yet — six thousand dollars and more" ' — but it's a formal gesture, in keeping with the quick tightening of loose nuts at this point and, in any event, Huck never returns to St Petersburg. As we have seen Twain was by this time unwilling to press home his social critique and so the issue is lost as the story tumbles towards its period a dozen lines later. His implicit comment nevertheless continues to lie there in Huck's scene with Judge Thatcher and should raise questions in our minds.

The dehumanising aspects of the Southern cash nexus are related of course in an integral way to the violence we shall discuss presently. It underpins the most grotesque brutality of all: the institutionalised chattelism which, I have argued, is the novel's primary focus. The licit cruelty and mercenariness of this system, Twain suggests, are the factors corrupting and morally destroying everyone who comes into contact with it. Not only is a choking cloud of violence released into the social air but people appear to lose the capacity to recognise one another as sentient fellow creatures. One planter wrote: 'It is a pity that agreeable to the nature of things Slavery and Tyranny must go together and that there is no such thing as having an obedient and useful Slave, without the painful exercise of undue and tyrannical authority.', (Stampp, p.141.) Other witnesses reported cases of sexual abuse, torture and even castrations:

> The angry mobs who dealt extra-legal justice to slaves accused of serious crimes committed barbarities seldom matched by the most brutal masters. 'They call it Lintch's Law,' wrote a frightened Louisiana plantation mistress during a local insurrection panic. 'If they continue hanging, as they have done for some time past, we should be careful of the children, otherwise the World might be left without people.' Fear turned groups of decent white men into ferocious mobs — fear and the knowledge that the law was not strong enough to touch them.
>
> (*The Peculiar Institution*, p.190.)

Twain comes close to giving expression to the particular feel and atmosphere of these mobs as we shall see, but he is also concerned to show what sorts of effect living in this kind of *milieu* has on ordinary people. So, for example, we see the lovely and gentle Wilks sisters, in many ways the most decent people Huck meets, treating their hare-lipped sister with merciless insensitivity. She is socially ostracised, rebuked publicly for her little failings, excluded from the family table and made to eat in the kitchen alone or with the servants. (Henry Nash Smith says that the scene with Joanna Wilks — Harelip — is just an instance of tasteless Twainian humour, but the situation is evidently more complex than this.) The ferry-boat owner delays setting out to help drowning people until he thinks he is assured of his payment. And of course there are almost no depths to which the king and the duke will not sink in pursuit of even a small pecuniary advantage.

Twain is dramatising a concept very close to the Marxian notion of alienation: a situation where individuals cease to perceive one another as individuals but regard them and themselves as expressions of monetary value alone. Thus an employer views his 'hands'

97

as a source of profit only, while the employees are compelled to market their labour power in competition with others. That is, they are alienated from their employer, who is only a source of wages; they are alienated from their fellow workers, who pose a threat to their own earnings; they are alienated from what they produce, since it is only the means of earning wages and not an end in itself; and they are alienated from themselves, since they are forced to view themselves as marketable commodities. I am not suggesting, of course, that Twain's analysis of human relations in *Huckleberry Finn*, however deformed he shows them as being, is anything like as schematic as this. Nevertheless, he reveals an awareness that the presence of the cash nexus is a perverting factor, an influence that makes it possible — especially in the violent context of the deep South — for anyone to perform almost any kind of brutality or cruelty upon any other. This applies especially in the area of white/black relations but, as can be seen in the cases of Sherburn and Boggs and the violent climaxes to the career of the king and the duke, by no means exclusively.

A striking example of alienation in action is the way Jim is treated after being recaptured by the Phelpses at the end of the novel:

> The men was very huffy, and some of them wanted to hang Jim, for an example to all the other niggers around there, so they wouldn't be trying to run away, like Jim done, and making such a raft of trouble, and keeping a whole family scared most to death for days and nights. But the others said, don't do it, it wouldn't answer at all, he ain't our nigger, and his owner would turn up and make us pay for him, sure.
>
> (*Huckleberry Finn*, Chapter 42.)

Humane considerations hardly enter into it, if at all. Were Jim the Phelpses' nigger, so the implication goes, he might well be strung immediately from the nearest tree. Huck adds with unconscious irony (though obviously here Twain is addressing simultaneously both his subjective and objective audiences, but at different levels):

> So that cooled them down a little, because the people that's always most anxious for to hang a nigger that hain't done just right, is always the very ones that hain't the most anxious to

pay for him when they've got their satisfaction out of him.

(Huckleberry Finn, Chapter 42.)

These sharply bitter passages – the bitterness is of course Twain's not Huck's – dramatise the way in which the white men are wholly alienated from Jim, seeing him only as a troublesome and ungrateful nigger, that is, irksome beast of burden, rather than as the human being he is. Moreover, the way Huck manages to find a general principle in the situation – the people that's *always* most anxious to hang a nigger is *always* the ones least anxious to pay – is a chilling reminder that this kind of event was by no means occasional. So the tormented black this time lives on only because of the high cost of dying – to his would-be murderers. (Eight hundred dollars is rather too much to pay for the 'satisfaction' of a hanging, even if the cost were to be shared around.)

Still, there remains the pleasure of a little assaulting – that comes free. 'They cussed Jim considerble. . .and give him a cuff or two, side of the head, once in a while.' Finally they chain him hand and foot to a staple driven through his cell floor. He is sentenced to a diet of bread and water and an indeterminate period of solitary confinement. Armed guards are to be posted at his prison door at night, and a bull-dog tethered there during the day.

And then they relent. The kindly doctor who tended Tom reveals that Jim's loyalty to the white boy probably saved his life. 'I tell you gentlemen,' he declares, expressing himself in the only terms that have meaning in this alienated universe, 'a nigger like that is worth a thousand dollars – and kind treatment, too.' They all agree, and realise that Jim deserves some sort of reward; so his sentence is commuted. 'Every one of them promised, right out and hearty, that they wouldn't cuss him no more. Then they come out and locked him up.'

The juxtaposition of these two sentences, and of course the hypocritical meaninglessness of the white men's promise, is wholly deliberate on Twain's part. Jim has saved Tom's life at the expense of his own freedom and he wins the right not to be verbally abused by people who are just about to go home anyway. Twain of course implies a parenthetical exclamation point after Huck's remark. And then, in case one has overlooked the irony, he makes Huck add:

I hoped they was going to say he could have one or two of the

99

chains took off, because they was rotten heavy, or could have meat and greens with his bread and water, but they didn't think of it. . .

(*Huckleberry Finn*, Chapter 42.)

Strikingly enough, Huck himself says nothing. The mood of the whites is still ugly and he is intimidated. 'I reckoned it warn't best for me to mix in, but I judged I'd get the doctor's yarn to Aunt Sally, somehow or other. . .'

What lies behind this episode is the disintegration and collapse of the system of chattel slavery. The reason the whites are so brutal and murderous is that they are in a posture of defensiveness. Earlier in the novel we learned that slaves are escaping, in ever increasing numbers, often singly but occasionally in batches of five or more (Chapter 16.).

Again, the historians bear out the accuracy of Twain's observations. Both Stampp and Genovese offer profiles of the typical runaway, and, in a word, he is Jim – an adult male in his prime, aged between sixteen and thirty-five, who suddenly makes off after a history of good relations with his owner. The cause was usually a single grievance. About a thousand slaves a year ran away during the 1850s, and 80 per cent came into this category. Moreover, the season of Jim's abrupt departure was also the one characteristically chosen by escaping blacks:

Runaways usually went singly or in small groups or two or three. But some escaped in groups of a dozen or more, and in a few instances in groups of more than fifty. They ran off during the warm summer months more often than during the winter when sleeping out of doors was less feasible and when frost-bitten feet might put an end to flight.

(*The Peculiar Institution*, p. 111.)

The excessively brutal behaviour of the whites at the Phelps plantation, however, is not be understood only in terms of the internal fissures appearing in the chattel system. Dispassionately considered, we could say that the Phelpses and their friends over-react in allowing their blood to be curdled by the silly letters Tom sends them. 'Beware. Trouble is brewing. Keep a sharp look-out. UNKNOWN FRIEND.' And, 'Don't betray me, I wish to be your friend. There is a desprate gang of cutthroats

100

from over the Ingean Territory going to steal your runaway nigger tonight, and they have been trying to scare you so as you will stay in your house and not bother them. I am one of the gang, but have got religgion and wish to quit it and lead an honest life again, and will betray the helish design.' (Chapter 39.)

However, this aspect of the evasion sequence at least is not seriously burlesqued by Twain. The slaveholders at this time actually were extremely jumpy and nervous, ready to be stampeded as they are in *Huckleberry Finn.* Genovese quotes Ulrich Bonnell Phillips: 'Many men of the South thought of themselves and their neighbours as living above a loaded mine, in which the negro slaves were the powder, the abolitionists the spark, and the free negroes the fuse.' (*Roll, Jordan, Roll*, pp. 398-9.) In other words, Twain acquaints us with the texture and feel of a typical insurrection panic.

Stampp argues persuasively that Southern white consciousness was dominated by Nat Turner's rebellion of August, 1831. Over a two-day period Turner and seventy followers marched through the Southampton countryside, killing nearly sixty whites. Turner was no Spartacus, however, and he and his small band were quickly crushed. There followed what we have learned to call a backlash: after summary trials the rebels were slaughtered and many others, even those only slightly implicated in their revolt — for example, those who might have expressed sympathy — were executed also or transported. Stampp sums it up well:

> Thus ended an event which produced in the South something resembling a mass trauma, from which the whites had not recovered three decades later. The danger that other Nat Turners might emerge, that an even more serious insurrection might some day occur, became an enduring concern as long as the peculiar institution survived.

(*The Peculiar Institution*, p. 134.)

Turner's had not been the first slave rebellion. It was not the last. In 1822 Denmark Vesey headed a complex conspiracy of some magnitude which came to nothing after it was betrayed. Savage reprisals, as always, followed its discovery. In 1835, following an insurrection panic in Mississippi and Louisiana, numerous slaves were executed; on another occasion in the same region the heads of sixteen slaves were impaled along the banks of the Mississippi as a warning. (Stampp, p. 135.) The sequence of revolts, small and large, continued throughout the existence of slavery, and came to something of a climax with the rebellion led by John Brown in 1859.

This, then, is the context of the Phelpses' reaction to the plans to liberate Jim. Twain's comment that they considered hanging him 'for an example to all the other niggers around there' thus would have echoed in a chamber of meaning and implication both for his Northern and Southern readerships.

The Religion of Violence

The discussion so far leads to an important truth about *Huckleberry Finn,* namely that the geographical and socio-historical detail it embraces are not to be separated in any sensitive reading. Twain's eye (and ear) for the definitive extended easily from the natural to the sociological and back again (we noticed him at in the 'loafers' passage earlier) in a rich interplay. He understood how each built dialectically upon the other for he was, in the philosophic sense, instinctively a materialist.

Huckleberry Finn thus represents a complex coming-together of disparate forces at work on Twain's talented pen. As we noted earlier, he had set out to create a sequel to *Tom Sawyer,* basing the new adventures on the roguish and slightly pathetic village scamp of that novel. Huck was originally a means of defining small-town respectability by displaying the consequences of its absence. His life was a justification, in Twain's eyes, for the restrictiveness of middle-class child-rearing:

> Shortly Tom came upon the juvenile pariah of the village, Huckleberry Finn, son of the town drunkard. Huckleberry was cordially hated and dreaded by all the mothers of the town, because he was idle and lawless and vulgar and bad − and because all their children admired him so, and delighted in his forbidden society, and wished they dared be like him. Tom was like the rest of the respectable boys, in that he envied Huckleberry his gaudy outcast condition, and was under strict orders not to play with him. So he played with him every time he got a chance. Huckleberry was always dressed in the castoff clothes of full-grown men, and they were in perennial bloom and fluttering with rags. His hat was a vast ruin with a wide crescent lopped out of its brim; his coat, when he wore one, hung nearly to his heels and had the rearwards buttons far down the back; but one suspender supported his trousers; the seat of his trousers bagged low and contained nothing; the

fringed legs dragged in the dirt when not rolled up.

Huckleberry came and went, at his own free will. He slept on doorsteps in fine weather and in empty hogs-heads in wet; he did not have to go to school or to church, or to call any being master or obey anybody; he could go fishing when and where he chose, and stay as long as it suited him; nobody forbade him to fight; he could sit up as late as he pleased; he was always the first boy that went barefoot in the spring and the last to resume leather in the fall; he never had to wash, nor put on clean clothes; he could swear wonderfully. In a word, everything that goes to make life precious, that boy had. So thought every harassed, hampered, respectable boy in St Petersburg.

(The Adventures of Tom Sawyer, Chapter 6.)

Twain's point of view in this novel is remorselessly bourgeois, expressing itself not only in terms of content but of course also in form. Consider for instance the plush Victorian verbiage of 'juvenile pariah' and 'the last to resume leather' – euphemisms completely foreign both to Twain and *Huckleberry Finn*. Moreover, as Twain's last-quoted sentence suggests, part of Tom Sawyer describes the assimilation of Huck into the Southern middle class and, as we know, Twain took this situation as his starting point for the later novel. The congruence of pressures we have already noticed, however, immediately began transforming his work. It became a genuinely indigenous fiction rather than something constructed analogically to the British tradition. Soon after settling down to write Twain was led into an examination of the meaning and significance of his own boyhood and adolescence; he became increasingly aware that the slavery issue in the South had not, in fact, been resolved during the first decade of Reconstruction; he found that he was able to draw on unexpectedly rich resources of natural, historical and liguistic information; and he seems, in this period, to have become more and more conscious of the creative dependence each had upon the other. What he finally produced was a critically-defined image of the pre-war Southern river culture.

For example, Huck rarely introduces a gratuitous piece of information about the Mississippi, despite the fact that Twain's main interest was clearly the life in the towns along its banks. Yet he contrives to amass an astounding wealth of natural detail in the process. The accuracy of his eye, which incidentally is completely persuasive, bolsters our confidence in his social witness. We learn, for instance, that tow-heads are sand-bars in the river that have cotton-woods upon them 'as thick as harrow-teeth' (Chapter 12). They can be up to sixty yards long, while some are so big they seem almost little islands, taking you – Twain's characteristic drive for typicality and representativeness addresses the reader in this intimate fashion – perhaps ten minutes to pass as you float by on a current pushing along at sometimes five miles an hour. Yet they are not so vast as the real islands, which may be five or six *miles* in length and over half-a-mile wide. And the river itself is correspondingly impressive; never less than a mile across, it is frequently one-and-a-half or two miles wide and, after the spring flooding that follows the first rains, occasionally 'a good many miles' from bank to bank (Chapter 9). It is more than eleven hundred miles long.[1]

Huck never introduces these facts in a goggle-eyed way. He himself is unimpressed by them, they are the every-day circumstances of his existence. Twain, on the other hand, has clearly placed them there for a purpose; he wishes to communicate the very nerve and marrow and bone of his South and that, finally, meant the big, dominating personality of the river. The detail he accumulates is part of this endeavour. It is the old dialectical principle of quantity transforming quality in action: the sheer weight and abundance of natural fact affects the whole timbre of the work.

We readers, however, especially if we are not American, have to glean this information from the off-hand references and casual remarks Twain allows both Huck and the other characters to throw out. Yet even if we do not consciously do this we cannot fail but be impressed by the river's power and strength, or ponder the manner in which its occasionally oppressive presence has shaped for good or ill the way life was and indeed is still lived along its shores. For instance, we discover with surprise that

[1] I would like to acknowledge my debt at this point to an outstanding but unpublished essay on *Huckleberry Finn* by Nigel Gray, my friend and former student. It was 25,000 words long and one of the best discussions of the book I have ever read. My whole conception of the novel, especially in this section, has been shaped by my recollection of it.

dwellings along the bank have to be built three of four feet above the ground on stilts to avoid being suddenly washed away by the spring rise. Yet so unpredictable are the effects of the flood, and so great its force, that sometimes whole strips of land, 'as wide as a house', will abruptly collapse. The thing is so common an occurrence that, as we have already seen, Huck is able to draw on it for a striking metaphor — 'Blamed if the king didn't have to brace up mighty quick, or he'd a squashed down like a bluff bank that the river has cut under. . .'. Worse: there are summers when entire sections of the riverside up to a quarter mile deep will crumble slowly like gingerbread into the water, home after home, dragging people and all they own with it (Chapter 21). Drownings are therefore frequent. At one point Huck and Jim come upon a two-storey wooden frame-house floating down stream 'tilted over considerble', with a naked, dead body inside. That they react so matter-of-factly of course speaks more loudly than any comment about the ordinariness of the experience. They ransack the house and go off gleefully with their plunder like little pirates (Chapter 9).[1] Subsequently, when Huck is trying to alert the ferry-boat owner to the dangers confronting the stranded *Walter Scott* — he invents a graphic lie about deaths and drowning — the man is quite unruffled and makes sure of his payment before setting out on what is obviously, to him, only another midnight rescue mission (Chapter 13).

These vivid dramatisations, on the one hand, give Twain's portrayal of life in the Mississippi basin its three-dimensional quality. He concretises, by his posture of representativeness and typicality, the most ordinary facets of daily living. And he does it always by contextualising and uncovering their human and social significance. But on the other hand he is also concerned to discover, and then communicate, the larger-than-life and almost mythological force he identifies with the river itself. What he does throughout the tale is to contrast and counterpose, at both a literal and quasi-symbolic level, the world of the waters and the

[1] It is only much later, towards the story's end, that we discover an additional significance in this encounter. The Barlow knife and fish-hooks Huck retrieves in fact constitute his only patrimony, and that without intention: the corpse was Pap's. The sordid conditions of his death — the place was obviously a brothel and a gambling den — compels a second thought then about Huck's own future as he prepares to move on.

world of the surrounding banks. On the whole, the river is a place of refuge, a place of tranquility where Huck and Jim are able to shed their shore-acquired clothing, as they do in one scene, and rediscover their common humanity. (There was more than a touch of the anarchist about Twain.) They become, like Lear, unaccomodated men. Their conversations range across the universe. What was the origin of the stars? Were they laid by the moon? What are the responsibilities of parents? Was Solomon, in his famous judgment over the disputed child, really wise? (Jim gives a negative answer in terms which closely approximate the modern commonsense portrayed in Brecht's *Caucasian Chalk Circle*.) When the fogs and dangers of the river descend the two grow even closer together — more like mother and child than, as Fiedler suggests in *Love and Death in the American Novel*, as lovers.

Alternatively, the white-dominated racist world they slide past is, precisely, the locus of the violence and meanness and grasping pettiness which both are seeking to escape. After each major episode ashore (the St Petersburg chapters, the Grangerford-Shepherdson feud, the Wilks sequence, the Sherburn encounter, and so forth) Huck and Jim retreat again to the freedom of the current until, at the Phelpses, they can retreat no further. Then Huck lights out for the Territory.

Twain does not regard the river, of course, as an American Eden. Although it is, in its grand neutrality, the place where peace and freedom can be found — at least temporarily — it is also, in its vastness, capable of immense cruelty and destructiveness. The point is, however, that its brutishness has an impersonal and democratic character. The real violence comes from the shores. Emissaries of cruelty invade it throughout the tale, craft-borne from the banks and driven by intelligences warped by racism and greed.

Again, Twain makes this tangible and visual by the concrete specificity of his observation. He places before us all the variety and complexity of the river's teeming traffic, from small boats, scows and logs crudely strung together — anything, in fact, that will bear weight — to the armed skiff that comes looking for Huck's drowned body. We discover that there were huge trading rafts in those days, with working crews of up to thirty men. They slept in six-bunk wigwams distributed around the deck and cooked their food on an open camp-fire in the middle. Something of the colossal proportions of these rafts can be gathered from Huck's casual remark that 'a little section' he finds floating down stream is twelve feet wide and nearly sixteen feet long. Such vast platforms, which are 'as long going by as a procession', were manoeuvred by batteries of sweeps, four at each end, and their captains proudly hoisted flags from the tall poles at front and back. 'It *amounted* to something being a raftsman on such a craft as that.' And then beyond the rafts were the great paddle steamers, the tyrants and lords of this river, pushed along by huge thirty-foot wheels. To the small-town bourgeoisie they were the outside world; but to Huck and Jim they are monsters of destruction: 'big and scary, with a long row of wide-open furnace doors shining like red-hot teeth. . .' Their crews are often arrogant and vicious, thinking it a great jest to run down lesser craft. Again Huck offers this observation as representative and typical:

> She aimed right for us. They often do that and try to see how close they can come without touching; sometimes the wheel bites off a sweep, and then the pilot sticks his head out and laughs, and thinks he's mighty smart.

> (*Huckleberry Finn*, Chapter 16.)

Huck describes vividly the smash, the splintering of the raft, the shouts and bells to stop the engines of the steamer. But then he cynically adds: 'of course that boat started her engines again ten seconds after she stopped them, for they never cared much for raftsmen. . .'

As far as the crew and passengers are concerned, Huck and Jim might as well be dead — drowned, crushed by the paddle perhaps, or struggling crippled and bleeding to the shore. In fact we are all led at this point to believe that Jim actually has been killed. The sequence is worth considering, for although Twain underplays it in practice — he moves his story along, gets Huck to the bank, throws him among the Grangerfords — it sets in relief one of the central features of his attitude towards the South. This is a vicious and destructive society, and Twain is both sickened by it and hostile towards it.

My point is that Twain frequently portrays the shore reaching out with bloody hands towards the peaceful stream. We twice encounter bounty hunters looking for niggers; we hear the thieves plot murder, and then face drowning, on the stranded

Walter Scott; the Grangerford boys are slaughtered from the banks as they struggle to climb out; and the duke and the king come again and again, in their moral and physical oppressiveness, to take over what is for Huck and Jim, after all, a very habitable world. They eventually betray them to the real, that is the human and legal, violence of the land.

What we are ultimately left with is a Twainian addition to what had become, even as early as the mid-1880s — Henry James had published his first novel more than ten years before — standard conventions of contrasted innocence and experience in the American novel. In Cooper the imaged antinomies accrete around the ideas of the frontier and the town; later writers, such as Melville and Hawthorne, brought to it such oppositions as east and west, rurality and urbanity, deviousness and frankness and, finally, especially though not exclusively in the work of Henry James, the ambiguous conflict between America and Europe.[1] In the world of *Huckleberry Finn* Twain locates these antagonisms on the river and on the shore, resolving the conflict unsatisfactorily, as we have argued, though always with the strong, if cynical, suggestion that society usually triumphs. On the other hand, of course, the individual — Huck — is invariably in the right.

The river, then, is nasty, brutish and huge. Twain's narrative tactic in dealing with this, however, is to define its implicit meaning in relation to the way life was actually lived in the settlements and harbours along its banks. And he does this, as we have noted, by adopting the posture of radical objectivity, by undertaking to give witness, in an almost total way, to the most banal but also the most revealing details of human existence at that time and place.

Huck describes a thunderstorm, a dawn, a night, a day, the sudden descent of fogs. Each is offered as a *typifying* moment. He reminds us of the way voices at night carry for miles over water, that when we watch someone chopping wood at a distance the *k'chunk*! of the blow arrives several seconds after we see the act. He tells us how deep and impenetrable a Southern night can seem, how the morning breeze above the Mississippi is filled with the mingled smell of dead fish and flowers, and how terrifyingly

[1] I have discussed this tradition more fully in *Henry James: The Ibsen Years* (London: Vision Press, 1972; New York: Barnes and Noble, 1973).

opaque a river mist can be. The silence before dawn is broken only by the 'cluttering' of bull-frogs; then –

> The first thing to see, looking way over the water, was a kind of dull line – that was the woods on t'other side – you couldn't make nothing else out; then a pale place in the sky; then more paleness, spreading around; then the river softened up, away off, and warn't black any more but gray; you could see little dark spots drifting along, ever so far away – trading scows and things; and long black streaks – rafts; sometimes you could hear a sweep screaking; or jumbled up voices, it was so still and sounds come so far; and by and by you could see a streak on the water which you know by the look of the streak that there's a snag there in a swift current which breaks on it and makes that streak look that way; and you see the mist curl up off the water, and the east reddens up, and the river, and you make out a log cabin in the edge of the woods, away on the bank on t'other side of the river, being a wood-yard, likely, and piled by them cheats so you can throw a dog through it anywheres; then the nice breeze springs up, and comes fanning you from over there, so cool and fresh and sweet to smell, on account of the woods and the flowers; but sometimes not that way, because they've left dead fish laying around, gars, and such, and they do get pretty rank; and next you've got the full day, and everything smiling in the sun, and the song-birds just going it!

(*Huckleberry Finn*, Chapter 19.)

This unforgettable passage rests on its specificity. The accumulating details, often unromantic in themselves, gather force and momentum as the earth spins towards the sun. Twain's prose moves with the dawn, increasing in intensity and excitement like a tone poem – Debussy's *La Mer*, for instance – engaging all our senses in succession: first our eyes, peering into the gloom; then moments of colour followed by the cool wind on our cheeks; then the bad and sweet smells; and, finally, the wildly chirping birds. And all the while Huck's stance is that of cicerone and instructor. This is the way it usually is, he says.

He tells us how to build a wigwam on a raft, and how to construct a safe fire inside it – on a layer of dirt at least five inches deep with a frame around to hold it in place. We are taught how to hang a night lantern and when, why to make an extra steer-age oar, which craft will help you, and when up-stream boats will seek out the easy water rather than the down-stream channel. We discover that Mississippi catfish can be more than six feet long and weigh well over two hundred pounds. They can only be caught with fishing lines as thick as a boy's finger and, as one might have expected, with 'monstrous' hooks. But it is worth the effort and the danger, especially if you are one of the poor. The meat is white and tasty, and can be sold by the pound at any of the nearby villages.

Twain's consciousness of what it meant to be poor adds depth and wholeness to his total picture. Again his ability to uncover the human significance in the most ordinary events is what gives his record its simultaneous status as fine documentary and great fiction. In fact the two are inseparable. We learn, for instance, that after the spring rains logs, rafts and bits of rafts, and, as we saw earlier, even wooden houses, are washed suddenly down stream. These bare facts, however, acquire vitality and social point when we discover in the same breath what such events can mean for the poor who, like Huck, are able to sell what they recover. A fourteen-foot canoe, which by Mississippi standards is only average, is worth as much as $10 – a considerable bonus in a society where a black man thinks of $14 as untold riches.[1] Huck

[1] Twain was careful to record the relative cash value of almost all com-modities in the antebellum South, for he recognised that money and not man was the measure of much that was there, including human life. Again, the impulse that led him into this kind of detail seems to have been the desire to deal in fictional form with a complete culture, in all its elegance and ugliness. We learn, as kind of reference point, that steamboat captains earned up to $60 a month, and were considered affluent. The king is thus comprehensibly pleased with the proceeds of a single day's graft exploiting religious emotions: nearly $90, together with the implied moral that crime pays – and you can choose your own hours. But cheating the locals out of their small change adds up too, and may be even more lucrative. The price of admission to the grand Shakespearean revival is 25c – for white adults. Children and niggers are allowed only 10c, one of Twain's striking details that says almost everything that need be said about day-to-day Southern racism. For the obscene show the charge is doubled (and of course the unpeople of the village, blacks, children and women, are excluded). And the taking are impressive: a cool $465 for three nights' work (Chapters, 21, 22.). We can see, then, that the king and duke are hardly victims of this system, in a material sense. Twain's real target is a way of life that makes it worth their while consistently to risk physical assault, and perhaps even death, in order to continue living freely.

at this juncture, also tells us something about the heartless toying with others' poverty, and what passes for humour in this world. As we shall see, it is entirely in keeping with what he later reveals about the rest of his social *milieu*. When he rows out to retrieve a prize canoe he says: 'I just expected there'd be somebody laying down in it, because people often do that to fool folks, and when a chap had pulled a skiff out most to it they'd raise up and laugh at him.' (Chapter 7.)

Huck's terminology here, incidentally, is worth noting as evidence of social attitudes. 'People' are reasonably affluent whites – Tom Sawyer's family, for example. 'Folks,' on the other hand, are destitute, like Pap Finn. Niggers, of course, are neither folks or people. When Huck is posing as Tom, he tells Aunt Sally that his steamer was involved in an accident. She says: 'Good gracious! Anybody hurt?' – 'No'm. Killed a nigger.' – 'Well it's lucky,' Twain allows the good-hearted woman to reply, ramming the point home, 'because sometimes people do get hurt.' (Chapter 32.)

Twain was, in fact, continually aware of social inequity, of the very poor and of the harsh conditions of their existence. When he visited England for the first time he was appalled at the exploitation of the working class and maintained thereafter – correctly, as Genovese has shown – that Southern blacks were often materially better off than 'free' white workers in London and Manchester. In *Huckleberry Finn*, Twain makes the same point with his characteristically acid humour. Huck, posing as the the king's English servant, is quizzed about conditions by Joanna Wilks, the hare-lipped daughter:

'. . .How is servants treated in England? Do they treat 'em better'n we treat our niggers?'

'*No*! A servant hain't nobody there. They treat them worse than dogs.'

'Don't they give 'em holidays, the way we do, Christmas and New Year's week, and Fourth of July?'

'Oh, just listen! A body could tell *you* hain't ever been to England, by that. Why, Hare-l – why, Joanna, you never see a holiday from year's end to year's end; never go to the circus, nor theatre, nor nigger shows, nor nowheres.'

(*Huckleberry Finn*, Chapter 26.)

112

This passage has sometimes been taken as satire. In fact, despite the humorous ambience, it is a bare declaration of truth.

In the same spirit Twain describes the main features of white working class existence in the South, offering several telling details as evidence. Their houses are shabby and rat-infested, and of course they are forced to eat badly. When they have meat it is often unpalatable — tough, cold, reeking of damp cellars and tasting 'like a hunk of old, cold cannibal' (Chapter 33.) The slaves, naturally, fare even worse; their food can be distinguished from that given to the dogs only because it occasionally includes watermelon (Chapter 34).[1] All this is deliberately contrasted with the splendid living of the 'quality,' the Sherburns and Shepherdsons and Grangerfords (we have already referred to Huck's distant characterisation of an upper-class breakfast), and the more-than-adequate living of the small plantation owners like the Phelpses. Huck's thoughts about the low-grade food eaten by the destitute actually occur as he sits down to a meal at Uncle Silas's table.

The effect of these contrasts is to convey the overwhelming sense of a whole way of life, from the most to the least privileged census groups, being brought under the novelist's eye. In isolation they might have suggested nothing more than conventional toyings with the liberal-bourgeois consciences of Twain's New England readership; but in conjunction with his efforts to typify and represent, which they clearly supplement, they leave us with what amounts to an almost total picture. *Huckleberry Finn* is consequently a striking, if partial, refutation of E.M. Forster's class-bound remark that the very poor cannot possibly be dealt with in fiction. 'They are unthinkable, and only to be approached by the statistician or the poet.' (*Howards End*, Chapter 6.)

And the reason, of course, was that Twain had been there. It is what breathes life into every line, what gives vitality to his most

[1] Stampp, confirms Twain's observations, pointing out that Blacks were never given fresh meat, milk or eggs but were allowed only a weekly ration of corn-crib and bacon. (*The Peculiar Institution*, pp. 284-5.) On the other hand, they were at least fed three times a day. Genovese quotes this account from a contemporary British witness in 1842: 'I have seen in the factory in which I worked wives and mothers working from morning till night with only one meal; and a child brought to suck at them thrice a day. I have seen fathers of families coming in the morning and working till night, and having only one meal, or two at the farthest extent.' (*Roll, Jordan, Roll* p. 58.)

prosaic characterisations and details. Although a Langdon when he sat down to write his novel, and although wholly assimilated into the Hartford Nook Farm community by the time he had completed it, he was still sufficiently in touch with his former existence to be able to record it accurately and with unmatched integrity. In fact, it is likely that his new circumstances and class perspectives brought home to him afresh the meaning of real poverty and social deprivation. A small example may clinch the point. He and Livy were wealthy enough to hire, as indeed they did, a whole series of wet nurses for their children when she proved unable to breast feed. But Twain shows that he knew and recalled how the Southern poor had dealt with this problem, immensely complicated in a world without rubber teats, (as Nigel Gray pointed out) when he allows Huck to come unexpectedly upon a broken milk bottle with a rag stopper for a baby to suck. This graphic detail, like so many others in the novel, succeeds in evoking and establishing the quotidian grind of an entire segment of Huck's society.

It is my contention nonetheless that Twain's close focus on the materially deprived, represented throughout the book of course by Huck's and Jim's struggle to survive, is at one level only a means enabling him to penetrate the heart of the river culture. His concern is simultaneously to place the whole matter before us and dramatise its meaning so that a judgment can be reached.

This is of course not to say that Twain's own attitude is concealed in any way: he was objective, but radically so. His unambiguous conclusion was that the prewar South was a disgustingly violent society riven with religious and other hypocrisies. In the Grangerford sequence, as Tony Tanner points out (*The Reign of Wonder*, p. 157 ff.), he offers a striking image of his sense of the falsity beneath the public posturing of those infected with Sir Walterism:

> On a table in the middle of the room was a kind of lovely crockery basket that had apples and oranges and peaches and grapes piled up in it which was much redder and yellower and prettier than real ones is, but they warn't real because you could see where pieces had got chipped off and showed the white chalk or whatever it was, underneath.
>
> (*Huckleberry Finn*, Chapter 17.)

Tanner rightly takes this image as an inferential attack on Tom Sawyer's 'style,' and indeed on all the stylish absurdities, both personal and political, which Twain consistently opposes to Huck's compassion and sound common sense. But it has another implication too, something close to what we mean when we speak of gods with feet of clay. Twain is pointing to the corrupt and fundamentally morbid substructure which underpins Southern gentility.

In his view the lynchpin of this corruption was religion, and especially American churchianity. Twain was of course a militant agnostic — to Livy's despair and his own uneasy discomfort. Nevertheless, by the time he had completed *Huckleberry Finn* he was capable of this sort of comment to William Dean Howells about George Washington Cable (February 27, 1885):

> That 'But' is pointing towards his religion. You will never, never know, never divine, guess, imagine, how loathesome a thing the Christian religion can be made until you come to know and study Cable daily and hourly. Mind you, I like him; he is pleasant company; I rage and swear at him sometimes, but we do not quarrel; we get along mighty happily together; but in him and his person I have learned to hate all religions. He has taught me to abhor and detest the Sabbath-day and hunt up new and troublesome ways to dishonour it. . .
>
> (*The Portable Mark Twain*, pp. 761-2.)

Twain was not jesting. In *A Connecticut Yankee in King Arthur's Court*, his next novel, he depicted religion and the established church (Merlin and Catholicism) as the source of all evil and reaction. Their opposition to The Boss drives him to his bunker and contributes to the mass slaughter which is the story's period. In his final proclamation Hank declares the nation free: 'With the monarchy, its several adjuncts died also; wherefore there is no longer a nobility, no longer a privileged class, no longer an Established Church; all men are become exactly equal; they are upon one common level, and religion is free.'

Of course, a native of Hartford could not be expected to see beyond the possibilities of American democratic republicanism; Hank wishes to be nothing more than the first President of sixth-century England. But Twain himself went further, and in his last and most cynical anti-religious

115

fiction, *The Mysterious Stranger* (1916) shows Satan alone possessing intelligence and existence:

'Strange! that you should not have suspected years ago — centuries, ages, aeons, ago! — for you have existed, companionless, through all the eternities. Strange, indeed, that you should not have suspected that your universe and its contents were only dreams, visions, fiction! Strange, because they are so frankly and hysterically insane — like all dreams: a God who could make good children as easily as bad, yet preferred to make bad ones; who could have made every one of them happy, yet never made a single happy one; who made them prize their bitter life, yet stingily cut it short; who gave his angels eternal happiness unearned, yet required his other children to earn it; who gave his angels painless lives, yet cursed his other children with biting miseries and maladies of mind and body; who mouths justice and invented hell — mouths mercy and invented hell — mouths Golden Rules, and forgiveness multiplied seventy times seven, and invented hell; who mouths morals to other people and has none himself; who frowns upon crimes, yet commits them all; who created man without invitation, then tries to shuffle the responsibility for man's acts upon man, instead of honorably placing it where it belongs, upon himself; and finally, with an altogether divine obtuseness, invites this poor, abused slave to worship him!. . .'

(*The Portable Mark Twain*, pp. 742-3.)

In *Huckleberry Finn* Twain's attack on religionism is less to the foreground, but it is by no means less explicit. It is exemplified, for example, by the pious Miss Watson who 'grumbles' a little over her food before eating, and who invites her servants in for evening prayers but has, at the same time, no compunction about separating a man from his family when a quick profit is to be made. The Phelpses indulge a similar hypocrisy, coming in to Jim's prison 'every day or two to pray with him,' but want to hang him from the nearest tree as an example to other uppitty niggers after his escape and recapture.

Twain repeatedly dramatises the bloodthirsty nature of professed Christians. The supreme examples are those models of social and religious rectitude, the Shepherdsons and Grangerfords, who see no contradiction at all between their avowal of brotherly love and their actual conduct. They sing hymns to the Prince of Peace with their shotguns at hand. And as they ride home from Church *en famille* on Sundays they are capable of growing misty-eyed over Loving One's Neighbour as a safe abstraction, but keep a sharp look-out for the Shepherdsons just the same. At home they worship Emmeline's icon, turning her bedroom into a shrine to death and sharing in a cult of morbidity. It makes Huck shudder; their hypocrisy and obsession with dying give him 'the fan-tods'.

The aristocratic Grangerfords are the nobility of their world; and in *A Connecticut Yankee* this is how Twain depicted them:

> I will say this much for the nobility: that, tyrannical, murderous, rapacious, and morally rotten as they were, they were deeply and enthusiastically religious. Nothing could divert them from the regular and faithful performance of the pieties enjoined by the Church. More than once I had seen a noble who had gotten his enemy at a disadvantage, stop to pray before cutting his throat; more than once I had seen a noble, after ambushing and despatching his enemy, retire to the nearest wayside shrine and humbly give thanks, without even waiting to rob the body. There was to be nothing finer or sweeter in the life of even Benvenuto Cellini, that rough-hewn saint, ten centuries later. All the nobles of Britain, with their families, attended divine service morning and night daily, in their private chapels, and even the worst of them had family worship five or six times a day besides. The credit of this belonged entirely to the Church. Although I was no friend to that Catholic Church, I was obliged to admit this. And often, in spite of me, I found myself saying, 'What would this country be without the Church?'

(*A Connecticut Yankee in King Arthur's Court*, Chapter 17.)

Twain's sarcasm is too evident to require further emphasis. It highlights his entire attitude towards institutionalised religion in general.

Throughout the action of *Huckleberry Finn* Twain portrays public Christianity as a nauseating spectacle. The weeping and mourning at the Wilks funeral revolts Huck: 'I never see anything so disgusting.' The eye-rolling and 'goody-goody Amen' is nothing more than 'soul-butter and hogwash'; it is 'rot and slush' that is simply 'sickening.' (Chapter 25.) Elsewhere he shows, quite accurately, that religious emotions are easily and superficially aroused; they can be quickly evoked and then turned into a species of insane drivel by any skilful orator (including, a little later, the king):

'Oh, come to the mourners' bench! come, black with sin! (*amen*!) come, sick and sore! (*amen*!) come, lame and halt, and blind! (*amen*!) come, pore and needy, sunk in shame! (a-a-men!) come all that's worn, and soiled, and suffering! — come with a broken spirit! come with a contrite heart! come in your rags and sin and dirt! the waters that cleanses is free, the door of heaven stands open — oh, enter in and be at rest!' (*a-a-men! glory, glory, hallelujah!*)

And so on. You couldn't make out what the preacher said, any more, on account of the shouting and crying. Folks got up, everywheres in the crowd, and worked their way, just by main strength, to the mourners' bench, with the tears running down their faces; and when all the mourners had got up there to the front benches in a crowd, they sung, and shouted, and flung themselves down on the straw, just crazy and wild.

(*Huckleberry Finn*, Chapter 20.)

Twain's disgust is obvious; yet his description of this characteristic scene is not exaggerated. His atheism is apparent, but he does not need to go outside the actual and factual to express it. Drawing on eyewitnesses and citing them verbatim, Stampp gives us this comparable portrait of a camp meeting in South Carolina:

When the services began, a great crowd assembled around a wooden platform, the Negroes on one side and the whites on the other. On the platform stood four preachers, and between the singing of the hymns two of them exhorted the Negroes and two the whites, 'calling on the sinners. . .to come to the Savior, to escape eternal damnation!' Soon some of the white people came forward and threw themselves, 'as if overcome,' before the platform where the ministers received their confessions and consoled them. Around a white girl, who had fallen into a trance, stood a dozen women singing hymns of the resurrection. 'In the camp of the blacks is heard a great tumult and a loud cry. Men roar and bawl out; women screech like pigs about to be killed; many, having fallen into convulsions, leap and strike about them, so that they are obliged to be held down.' The Negroes made more noise and were more animated than the whites, but the behavior of the two races did not differ in any fundamental way. Except for condemning a 'holy dance' which some Negro women engaged in for a new convert, the whites did not appear to think that the Negroes acted in an outrageous or unchristian fashion.

(The Peculiar Institution, pp. 376-7.)

But it is what religion does to individuals that appals Twain most. Throughout the novel the two centres of political and social values are official churchianity and Huck's deepest impulses to humanity and compassion. The pivotal episodes result from the dramatised conflict between these struggling forces. Huck discovers increasingly that what he has been taught is at odds with himself and his experience of life, constricting his kindliness and demanding that he acquiesce in the evil notion that blacks can be the property of whites. (Even in the evasion sequence Twain refuses to let this point quite go. The persona Tom adopts in his bloodcurdling notes to the Phelpses declares that he is betraying his friends because he has 'got religgion.') Each time Huck wrestles with his conscience over what to do about Jim the struggle is in terms of what he sees and knows to be good — freedom, humanity, loyalty to friends — but what the Sunday School voices in his head tell him is bad. As he and Jim approach Cairo the confrontation becomes intense; Huck realises that he is helping a nigger to freedom, and all his education and religious training rise up in protest:

Conscience says to me, 'What had poor Miss Watson done to you, that you could see her nigger off right under her eyes and never say one single word? What did that poor old woman do to you that you could treat her so mean? Why, she tried to learn you your book, she tried to learn you your manners, she tried to be good to you every way she knowed how. That's what she done.'

(Huckleberry Finn, Chapter 16.)

A white boy who had helped a nigger escape would more likely fear the legal consequences of what he had done than fear for the fate of his soul. Every state provided severe penalties either for nigger stealing or for helping a slave to escape. Punishments ranged from long terms in prison to death. (Stampp, pp. 211, 198; Genovese, p. 655.) But Twain's emphasis at this point is on the role of religion in supporting the iniquitous system; so he has Huck dwell on his religious indoctrination (Miss Watson had learned him his book well).

Of course Twain is insisting on Jim's own claims to humanity; it is these which reduce to cant the sanctimony of the religionists. All of Huck's tortured queries could be put to him about Jim, too, and answered in the very same way. But Twain is making his point obliquely. By placing Huck in a crisis he is able to take us both into the very mentality of Southern racism ('Give a nigger an inch and he'll take an ell', Huck begins to think presently) and show how it is indissolubly linked to the moral and intellectual perversions of Southern Christianity.

On this occasion, as on all others, Huck's humanity triumphs over his miseducation. But then, as he disarmingly confesses, he was always a hopeless case. ('A sound heart and a deformed conscience come into collision', Twain wrote in his notes, 'and conscience suffers defeat.') When the slave hunters appear Huck just 'gives up trying' to be good — that is, betray his friend — and lies to them.

After they leave Huck is emotionally drained and depressed, and Twain makes his chief point: prejudice is unnatural and the consequence of early training. 'I see it warn't no use for me to try to learn to do right; a body that don't get *started* right when he's little, ain't got nothing to show — when the pinch comes there ain't nothing to back him to his work, and so he gets beat.' Huck's way out of this impasse is moral utilitarianism: he realises that if he had given Jim up he'd be feeling even worse now. 'Well, then, says I, what's the use you learning to do right, when it's troublesome to do right and ain't no trouble to do wrong, and the wages is just the same? I was stuck. I couldn't answer that. So I reckoned I wouldn't bother about it, but after this always try to do whichever came handiest at the time.' (Chapter 16.)

As Huck's remark shows, his strength is his pragmatism. At Miss Watson's urging he had tried prayer, because she said God would give him what he asked for, but nothing happened. 'I tried it. Once I got a fishline, but no hooks. It warn't any good to me

120

without hooks. I tried for the hooks three or four times, but somehow I couldn't make it work. By-and-by, one day, I asked Miss Watson to try for me, but she said I was a fool. She never told me why, and I couldn't make it out no way.' (Chapter 3.)

Yes, it's a joke; but like most of Twain's humour there is a serious face behind it. This moment in the novel comes straight out of an incident in Twain's own childhood. In one of the suppressed passages in his autobiography, subsequently salvaged and reprinted by Bernard Devoto in *Mark Twain in Eruption* (Grosset & Dunlap, New York, 1940, pp.108-9), Twain indicates that a similar experience marked a stage in his own progress towards unbelief. He had a Sunday School teacher called Miss Horr, 'a New England lady of middle age with New England ways and principles,' who told her class that 'whosoever prayed for a thing with earnestness and strong desire need not doubt that his prayer would be answered.' Ask, she told them, and ye shall receive.

Young Sam Clemens, 'struck by this information and. . . gratified by the opportunities which it offered, immediately put in an application for a slice of gingerbread. To his delight his prayer was answered.

> But this dream was like almost all the other dreams we indulge in in life, there was nothing in it. I did as much praying during the next two or three days as anyone in that town, I suppose, and I was very sincere and earnest about it too, but nothing came of it. I found that not even the most powerful prayer was competent to lift the gingerbread again, and I came to the conclusion that if a person remains faithful to his gingerbread and keeps his eye on it, he need not trouble himself about your prayers.

> *(Mark Twain in Eruption*, p. 109.)

After coming to a similar conclusion Huck even consults the Widow Douglas, who represents the spiritual arm of Christian hyprocrisy. What she has to say so contradicts Miss Watson's worldly pieties that he decides there must be 'two Providences, and a poor chap would stand considerable show with the widow's Providence, but if Miss Watson's got him there warn't no help for him any more.' After further reflection he decides logically and, from the radical perspective, completely accurately, that religion is just another tool of social oppression:

121

I went and told the widow about it, and she said the thing a body could get by praying for it was 'spiritual gifts.' This was too many for me, but she told me what she meant — I must help other people, and do everything I could for other people, and look out for them all the time, and never think about myself. This was including Miss Watson, as I took it. I went out in the woods and turned it over in my mind a long time, but I couldn't see no advantage in it — except for the other people — so at last I reckoned I wouldn't worry about it any more, but just let it go.

(*Huckleberry Finn*, Chapter 3.)

Huck discards chocolate-box Christianity but he is not without superstition. He still believes in God but in his final struggle with the preachers — when he tears up his letter to Miss Watson and sets out to rescue Jim himself — he comes literally to a damning resolution. The hell with it, he says. The victory, at this point, is of life over death, humanity over religion.

Still, Huck possesses an elaborate system of beliefs. Twain uses his account of them to take us deeper into the fabric of Southern society.

It is of course wholly a river culture, and Huck's vivid portrayal of its nature-myths interweaves superstition and truths in ways comprehensible to the modern social anthropologist. Levi-Strauss, for example, has argued in structuralist terms which nevertheless recall the Marxian concept of the relation between a society's economic base and its ideological superstructure, that social myths both arise from their host communities and then help to transform or sustain them. A myth or a superstition always has a practical or utilitarian point, even it it is only justifying the ways of social organisation to man.

Most of the legends and superstitions Huck details have accreted around the idea of death by water. For instance, he believes that a drowned man floats on his face, but a drowned woman floats on her back. Whether this is true or not, it helps him anticipate his father's return. We learn that bread filled with mercury is drawn to a corpse entangled along the bank, and that the concussion of cannon fired over water makes bodies come to the surface. The second is credible, the first obviously less so; but what both reveal together is the ingrained fear of the river, and sense of

122

dependence on it too, among the people who live there. T.S. Eliot called Huck's Mississippi a god; he must have been at least partly responding to the reverence with which it is seen to be treated in the novel. The search for Huck's corpse is not only death-worship or love for justice. As we shall see, bloody violence and sanctioned injustice, both expressed in the death of Boggs and its aftermath, are a commonplace in this society. It is only death by water that seems to call forth such elaborate, ritual behaviour.

Huck's fears and little rites, many of which he willingly acquires from Jim, help throw into relief the main outlines of lower-class life in the mid-nineteenth century South. And since this group – the slaves and the poor whites – were a substantial section of the total population, we may say that novels like *Huckleberry Finn* put us in touch, as no formal history has yet done, with the felt experience of Southern slavery. Gramsci remarks in *The Modern Prince* that commonsense is the practical wisdom of a ruling class. We may add, particularly on the basis of a novel like *Huckleberry Finn*, that folk-lore is the organised pragmatism of the peasantry.

Huck holds certain beliefs, for example, about the danger of glimpsing the moon over his shoulder, or spilling salt. While they clearly have no contact with reality, they do serve to emphasise the actual precariousness of his existence. They set him on his guard, and keep him there. Equally, it cannot be said that his rituals concerning warts are wholly impractical; modern medical research now suggests a psychosomatic element in the affliction (incidentally accounting for the success of faith-healing methods).

In the same way, most of Jim's lore is eminently practical. Birds *do* seek shelter before a storm, and it is likely that roast snake's skin and whiskey actually do combine to make a primitive serum. Genovese comments interestingly:

> The methods used by black herb doctors and conjurers ranged from the maddest quackery and outright charlatanry to pragmatically effective folk medicine. Not a few of the remedies found their way into the planters' own repertory for the good reason that they produced better results than available alternatives. Even some planters who were themselves doctors did not hesitate to turn to the black herb doctors for help. 'There's allus some old time nigger who knowed all dif'rent

kinds of yarbs and roots,' recalled Abram Sells of Texas, who insisted that his grandfather could stop bleeding and conjure away fevers and warts.

(Roll, Jordan, Roll, p. 227.)

By the same token poisonous snakes, dead or alive, are probably best left alone, so Jim's general taboo has survival value. (It has yet to be scientifically shown by ethologists that the mate of a dead rattlesnake really will come and curl herself around its body; but on the other hand it is credible, and also striking that the same lore is widespread among disparate cultures. Kipling, for instance, records a similar behaviour among cobras in his story *Riki-Tiki-Tavi*, and I was personally told the same thing about *boomslange* in South Africa.)

Huck of course offers little discrimination between fact and superstition in his account. His recipes for serum, his observations about the dead rattler's mate, and his belief in the general bad luck of handling snake skins, are all given in the same breath and at the same level of credulity. His attitude is like Pap's, who wears a cross in the heel of his shoe to ward off the devil: why take chances? The world through Huck's eyes is a continuum of ghosts and men; his only test is whether what he believes helps him to survive or not. His folklore is a mysterious mixture of the practical and the ridiculous:

> . . .I've always reckoned that looking at the new moon over your left shoulder is one of the carelessest and foolishest things a body can do. Old Hank Bunker did it once, and bragged about it; and in less than two years he got drunk and fell off the shot tower and spread himself out so that he was just a kind of layer, as you may say; and they slid him edgeways between two barn doors for a coffin, and buried him so, so they say, but I didn't see it. Pap told me. But anyway, it all come of looking at the moon that way, like a fool.

(Huckleberry Finn, Chapter 10.)

This is actually quite a complex passage in spite of its apparent innocence. First, as it illustrates, Twain's collection of folk beliefs and stories helped him to flesh out and give depth to his total picture. Stretchers like this one were utterly characteristic of the region. Secondly, Twain is able to establish Huck's pragmatic

124

credulity in touches such as these — the perfect vehicle, as it later becomes, for his deadpan humour. Thirdly, the tale of Hank Bunker reveals something about Huck's relationship with his father, who was evidently not above pulling his son's leg, as well as something about the self-deceiving nature of religious belief. And finally, the accumulation of such aparently random touches actually adds to Huck's authority as narrator and witness: he is obviously speaking from the very centre of his society. Huck, that is, Twain, is able to throw off almost effortlessly this kind of striking evidence of peasant superstitions and beliefs. Each one contributes a further dimension to the final social image.

Is it true that chickens know when it is going to rain? It hardly matters; what the detail really stresses is that this is a part of the world where it's important to know when the floods will come. It goes along with the memorable information that after the storms the river rises so severely its islands are engulfed. Moreover, the animals inhabiting them are forced to take to the trees and become so docile with hunger they can be touched and petted; excepting the snakes and turtles, who slip into the water and swim away. Surviving on the river dominates the education we receive from Huck; in fact, the novel often reads precisely like a survivor's manual. In this respect it comes close, again, to another classic of American fiction, *Moby Dick*.

Twain's final case against the antebellum South, however, is not just that it is shot through with religious hypocrisies and primitive superstitions. What he leaves us with is a picture of a world distraught with violence and gratuitous destruction, a society so contemptuous of human life that he ultimately turns away from it in disgust. The reason that Huck's little platitude about cruelty stands out so sharply ('Human beings *can* be awful cruel to one another.') is because of the mass of corroborating evidence that has gone before.

The most vivid and memorable illustration of this, as we have seen, is the feud sequence, and especially of course its bloody finale with the Shepherdsons baying 'kill! kill!' around the dying children. Twain emphasises the brutal, gratuitous lawlessness of it all:

> 'Well,' says Buck, 'a feud is this way. A man has a quarrel with another man, and kills him; then that other man's brother kills *him*; then the other brothers, on both sides, goes for one

another; then the *cousins* chip in — and by-and-by everybody's killed off, and there ain't no more feud. But it's kind of slow, and takes a long time.'

(Huckleberry Finn, Chapter 18.)

The killing ends when there is no one left. It is like a ghastly intuition of World War III. Twain points up the terrifying absurdity of it all by making a child describe the situation in simple, elemental words. Like ourselves, the Grangerfords and Shepherdsons mechanically prepare for war and await total and sudden destruction. By-and-by everybody's killed off. And every time 'a man died, or a woman died, or a child died,' the ghoulish Emmeline is at hand, like a military chaplain or some dreadful warpoet, with her 'tributes.'

'Has this one been going on long, Buck?'

'Well I should *reckon*! it started thirty year ago, or som'ers along there. There was trouble 'bout something and then a lawsuit to settle it; and the suit went agin one of the men, and so he up and shot the man that won the suit — which he would naturally do, of course. Anybody would.

(Huckleberry Finn, Chapter 18.)

Naturally. Like the equally aristocratic Sherburn, who guns down Boggs. Twain's point — 'Anybody would.' — is of course that in a civilised community nobody would. The purpose of a court adjudication is to settle disputes peacefully. In Buck's world, however, like a black joke from *Catch-22*, the loser up and shot the man that won. So the winner lost and the loser won. And so *ad infinitum* and, for Twain, *ad nauseam*. It is the Southern system. 'There is not a single celebrated Southern name in any of the departments of human history', he recorded in his notes, 'except those of war, murder, the duel, repudiation and massacre.'

'What was the trouble about, Buck? — land?'

'I reckon maybe — I don't know.'

'Well, who done the shooting? — was it a Grangerford or a Shepherdson?'

'Laws, how do *I* know? it was so long ago.'

'Don't anybody know?

'Oh, yes, pa knows, I reckon, and some of the other old

folks; but they don't know, now, what the row was about in the first place.'

(Huckleberry Finn, Chapter 18.)

After this amazing confession we have to remind ourselves that the sequence was not included lightly in the tale. We noted in the Introduction, for example, how Twain carefully sought direct evidence of Southern feuds when he made his return visit down the Mississippi in 1882 ('ask about old feuds.'), and the details of this one were actually taken from life. Twain, who in 1868 had said, 'I don't care anything about being humorous, or poetical, or eloquent, or anything of that kind — the end and aim of my ambition is to be authentic — to be considered authentic,' was most emphatic on this point. He told one reader, who had asked whether blood feuds really existed in the South, 'Yes, indeed, feuds existed in Kentucky, Tennessee and Arkansas, of the nature described, within my time and memory. I came very near being an eye-witness to the general engagement detailed in the book. The details are historical and correct.' (Cited by Blair, *Mark Twain and Huck Finn*, p. 225.) Huck's comment on the bloody climax, then, is also Twain's own:

It made me so sick I most fell out of the tree. I ain't agoing to tell *all* that happened — it would make me sick again if I was to do that. I wished I hadn't come ashore that night, to see such things. I ain't ever going to get shut of them — lots of times I dream about them.

(Huckleberry Finn, Chapter 18.)

Twain hardly stops there, however. He is able to draw a veil over that particular carnage because his novel is thick with other examples. (It will be remembered that one of the reasons the book was originally banned was because of its bloodiness.) The story's point, built up cumulatively, is that the brutality and bloodlust, the human degradation and disregard for suffering, are everywhere. Violence characterises Huck's universe. In *Life on the Mississippi*, the novel's contemporary and in many ways its companion volume, Twain described his own account of a gratuitous murder committed just below Memphis, as a 'piece of history illustrative of the violent style of some of the people down along here.' A similar preoccupation is a major theme in *Huckleberry Finn*.

Death or its threat is the climax of virtually every major or minor sequence in the novel. The St Petersburg chapters culminate in a night of horrible fright for Huck, who is trapped in a deserted woodshack with his drunk, murderous father:

> By-and-by he rolled out and jumped on his feet looking wild, and he see me and went for me. He chased me round and round the place, with a clasp-knife, calling me the Angel of Death and saying he would kill me and then I couldn't come for him no more. I begged, and told him I was only Huck, but he laughed *such* a screechy laugh, and roared and cussed, and kept on chasing me up. Once when I turned short and dodged under his arm he made a grab and got me by the jacket between my shoulders, and I thought I was gone; but I slid out of my jacket quick as lightning, and saved myself. Pretty soon he was all tired out, and dropped down with his back against the door and said he would rest a minute and then kill me. He put his knife under him, and said he would sleep and get strong, and then he would see who was who.

(*Huckleberry Finn*, Chapter 6.)

Huck escapes death by a fraction, and goes to sleep with a loaded gun pointed at his father's snoring body. He obviously intends to use it if he has to. When Pap goes off leaving him a prisoner, he resolves to fake his own death and escape.

Later, on Jackson's Island with Jim, the idyll is shattered by the news that armed bounty hunters are in pursuit. They have delayed their attack only long enough 'to borrow another gun'. Then, when Huck and Jim flee down river they encounter more bounty hunters; they come upon murder and treachery aboard the *Walter Scott* (which ends in the death of the would-be killers and their victim); and, finally, they themselves are smashed beneath the bows of the paddle steamer. The monster leaves them for dead.

The little scene tacked on to the end of the *Walter Scott* episode, like most of Twain's details, develops a related facet of Southern inhumanity. (It is like the treatment of Joanna, the hare-lipped Wilks sister, who is made to eat in the kitchen away from the family.) As far as the sleepy ferry-boat owner is concerned, the wet and frightened little boy shivering in front of him is telling the truth. Five people — Miss Hooker and her servant, and the boy's father, mother and sister — are trapped on board

128

the wreck and in the most terrible danger. One man, Bill Whipple, has already drowned and, as the boatman instantly appreciates, there isn't a moment to lose: 'Why, great goodness, there ain't no chance for 'em if they don't get off mighty quick!' But he inexplicably delays and delays before setting out to rescue them; and then he comes at last to the question that is really bothering him. 'Who in dingnation's agoing to *pay* for it?' It is only when Huck persuades him that Miss Hooker is related to Jim Hornback, the richest man in town, that he sets off. Twain is dramatising in this scene the essence of Southern alienation — the reduction of all human relationships to a function of the cash nexus. It is a theme that recurs throughout the action.

It is after this episode that Huck's and Jim's raft is run down in sport by the paddle steamer. When Huck clambers ashore he discovers that the Grangerfords' entire world is dominated by the imminence of abrupt and violent death. Later, when the king and the duke take over the raft, which is accomplished by a simple display of *force majeure*, they themselves are escaping lynchings. The brutality comes at Huck from every side.

The long sequence with the two rogues in command is, apart from the feeble evasion chapters, the least bloody in the novel. Nonetheless it is precisely here that we come upon Twain's most explicit analysis and condemnation of Southern violence. In a little one-horse town in Arkansas, chosen almost at random but also, as Twain makes clear, for its social representativeness and typicality, Huck witnesses the cold-blooded murder of the harmless and innocent Boggs.

Twain prepares for this climax skilfully, since it is not included for the sake of melodrama or literary swashbuckle. The incident is an integral part of his complete picture. Huck first gives little signals that tension is in the air: 'I seen three fights', he casually remarks of his tour through town. He then implies that violence is the only meaningful thing that happens in this dulled and vacuous provinciality. Again, it must be recalled that Huck is speaking not only of an incident, but of the sort of thing that *characteristically* occurs in these towns. A sow, he says, 'as happy if she was on salary', might happen to wander into the main street followed by her piglets and

pretty soon you'd hear a loafer sing out, 'Hi! *so* boy! sick him,

Tige!' and away the sow would go, squealing most horrible, with a dog or two swinging to each ear, and three or four dozen more a-coming; and then you would see all the loafers get up and watch the thing out of sight, and laugh at the fun and look grateful for the noise.

(*Huckleberry Finn*, Chapter 21.)

The cruel treatment of animals, which is completely mindless, is symptomatic of a general disregard for suffering and life. Twain's passage continues:

> Then they'd settle back again till there was a dog-fight. There couldn't anything wake them up all over, and make them happy all over, like a dog-fight — unless it might be putting turpentine on a stray dog and setting fire to him, or tying a tin pan to his tail and see him run himself to death.

(*Huckleberry Finn*, Chapter 21.)

What kind of society is this, Twain implies, where immolation is a jest and terror a distraction? His clear point is that there is little difference between this cruelty and the behaviour of the murderers on the *Walter Scott*, or the bounty hunters, or the steamer pilots who run others down for a laugh. They all exist on the same continuum. The whole sequence is capped, then, by the dramatic account of Boggs' murder.

Twain carefully establishes that Colonel Sherburn has only the slightest justification for his action: his larger point is that this kind of violence is ultimately indulged in almost for its own sake. Boggs could hardly be more inoffensive. He is 'the best-naturedest old fool in Arkansas — never hurt nobody, drunk nor sober', a man known for his harmless bluster. He is one of the town's characters, a living joke who goes on a blind drunk once a month. Sherburn, on the other hand, is the local aristocracy — his patrician airs, as Louis J. Budd remarks, suggest a ruined planter (*Mark Twain: Social Philosopher*, Indiana University Press, 1964, p.100). He is the wealthiest man in town, owner of the largest store, and is far and away the best-dressed man around.

Boggs' crime has been to accuse Sherburn of swindling his customers. Instead of rebutting the charge, however, as he might do were it untrue, Sherburn permanently silences his critic. Twain is of course implying that the duel thus dramatises the unequal

130

struggle between consumer and capitalist, between poor and rich. This is made even more apparent when we realise that Sherburn murders Boggs in spite of the fact that the terrified old man has actually complied with the ultimatum. At one o'clock, the deadline which, like an adolescent bully, Sherburn has challenged Boggs to cross, the old man is desperately silent. His final words are a frightened plea: 'O Lord, don't shoot!' Sherburn guns him down with contemptuous satisfaction anyway, and walks off, confident that he is above the law. In fact, he *is* the law. For Twain and the reader he incarnates Southern violence.

The crowd gathers round Boggs' still-warm body in the same way they might peer at the corpse of a charred dog. Their conduct clearly fills Twain with repugnance:

> Well, pretty soon the whole town was there, squirming and scrouging and pushing and shoving to get at the window and have a look, but people that had places wouldn't give them up, and folks behind them was saying all the time, 'Say, now, you've looked enough, you fellows; t'ain't right and t'ain't fair, for you to stay thar all the time, and never give nobody a chance; other folks has their rights as well as you.'
>
> (*Huckleberry Finn*, Chapter 21.)

Their right is the chance to look upon the face of death and consider the nemesis of those who cross Colonel Sherburn. Twain is of course conscious of the irony that it is only now that justice and fairness are invoked. No one raised a hand to defend Boggs. Nobody tried to stop the killing. The whole episode was treated as a spectacle. Now the crowd savour Bogg's dying to the full, watching again with a kind of lustful prurience as a lanky man in a white hat — Twain's image of himself, perhaps? — re-enacts the murder in all its grisly detail. 'The people that had seen the thing said he done it perfect; and said it was just exactly the way it all happened. Then as much as a dozen people got out their bottles and treated him.' Meanwhile Boggs' sixteen-year old daughter is weeping over the corpse.

The crowd's reaction is predictable and, as we discover, has been anticipated by Sherburn. He is a military man and this is a small campaign. The killing of Boggs is his challenge to the town, his assertion of his right, or at least his power, to do exactly as he pleases. Sensing this the crowd confronts him with a rope and the threat of a lynching; violence, in the South, as the Grangerford episode demonstrated, is met with even greater violence. No sheriff is asked for, or appears, or possibly even exists. Legal processes seem to be completely absent.

And Sherburn faces the people down. He makes clear what we had already guessed, especially from the anxious conduct of the king and the duke: lynchings, too, are common. Sherburn sneers: 'Because you're brave enough to tar and feather poor friendless cast-out women that come along here, did that make you think you had grit enough to lay your hands on a *man*?' The plural is chilling, and just sufficiently evocative of the New Testament story of the woman taken in adultery to make Twain's point, again, about the Christian hypocrisy of these people. But he probes more deeply than this, however, because in an oblique way he shares Sherburn's misanthropy. Like Sherburn Twain has the greatest contempt for oppressed or intimidated people who will not liberate themselves but actually acquiesce in their oppression by behaving with meekness and humility. His anger, however, is not Nietzschean; it is more like Robert Tressell's in *The Ragged-Trousered Philanthropists*, and emanates from the same radical impulse.

Sherburn, laughing in a way 'that makes you feel like when you are eating bread that's got sand in it,' rubs the crowd's nose in his contempt for them:

> 'Do I know you? I know you clear through. I was born and raised in the South, and I've lived in the North; so I know the average all around. The average man's a coward. In the North he lets anybody walk over him that wants to, and goes home and prays for a humble spirit to bear it. . .Now the thing for *you* to do, is to droop your tails and go home and crawl in a hole. If any real lynching's going to be done, it will be done in the dark, Southern fashion; and when they come they'll bring their masks, and fetch a *man* along.'
>
> (*Huckleberry Finn*, Chapter 22.)

Twain avoids an overt reference to the Ku-Klux Klan, which by the 1870s was already internationally notorious; but his meaning is clear.

Like the average man he is, Huck slinks away with the rest of the mob. 'I could a staid, if I'd wanted to, but I didn't want to.'

Later, however, Twain returns to this theme – the coward-liness which is the dialectical complement to Southern violence – when the king and the duke devise their strategem for protecting Jim in their absence. They paint him blue and dress him in ridiculous garb with the notice: 'Sick Arab – but harmless when not out of his head.' Huck's reaction looks back to Sherburn's speech and validates it:

> The duke told Jim to make himself free and easy, and if any-body ever come meddling around, he must hop out of the wigwam, and carry on a little, and fetch a howl or two like a wild beast, and he reckoned they would light out and leave him alone. Which was sound enough judgment; but you take the average man, and he wouldn't wait for him to howl. Why, he didn't only looked like he was dead, he looked considerably more than that.
>
> (*Huckleberry Finn*, Chapter 24.)

Sherburn then rebuts the threat of violence with an even greater threat; he holds a shotgun in his hands. Being a *man*, in the American Southwest, means to be able to out-terrorise terror. Critics who talk about his 'bravery' confronting the mob quite miss Twain's point, which is that there is little valour in an armed man facing an unarmed crowd of average men.

Later we discover what such a mob can do when it encounters helpless victims. The king and the duke are tarred, feathered, and run out of town on a rail. And it is then that Huck, and of course through him Twain, makes his effective statement about the cruelty of humankind. The truism strikes home with considerable force only because it is able to draw power and direction from what we have already witnessed. And in the same way it adds significance to the violent action that is the story's penultimate climax, the escape from the Phelps family and friends. *Huckleberry Finn* is a comedy that totters on the edge of tragedy.

The question we posed at the beginning of this section was whether literature could be reliable historical evidence. One answer is that it depends what you are looking for evidence of. But on the other hand, and in a more general way, we could say that on the basis of a novel like *Huckleberry Finn* literature is not only good evidence, but is in many respects indispensable evidence, if we are to arrive at a complete picture of a given moment in the social process. Formal histories, even accurate ones, are frequently impalpable or even dismissive and uninterested in the actual felt experiences of most of the people who were there. The best imaginative writing, on the other hand, is strong precisely in this area. Of course, this is not to say that the only function of literature is to witness with integrity; but in many crucial literary examples, of which *Huckleberry Finn* is one, to ignore such a dimension is to deform the text and ignore its context. Twain's novel is one of the very best histories of its period because it details and concretises, in an almost matchless way, the full experience of an entire way of life. It supplements, and in some cases completely replaces, the usual academic analyses. And it does this, above all, by being excellent in its own medium, by being superlative narrative fiction. The apparent paradox is the final twist to the Twainian dialectic.

Select Bibliography

S.L. CLEMENS: *Adventures of Huckleberry Finn* (San Francisco:Chandler Publishing Company, 1962) with an introduction and bibliography prepared by Hamlin Hill. (A Facsimile of the First Edition published in London by Chatto and Windus, 1884.) *The Adventures of Tom Sawyer* (London: Chatto and Windus, 1962; New York: Dell Publishing Company, 1972.) *A Connecticut Yankee in King Arthur's Court* (London: Chatto and Windus, 1967; New York: The Modern Library, no date.) *Mark Twain's Autobiography* (New York and London: Harper and Brothers, 1924) with an introduction by Albert Bigelow Paine, in two volumes.

WALTER BLAIR: *Mark Twain and Huck Finn* (Berkeley and Los Angeles: University of California Press, 1960.)

BERNARD DEVOTO: *The Portable Mark Twain* (New York: Viking Press; London: Chatto and Windus, 1965.) *Mark Twain in Eruption: Hitherto Unpublished Pages about Men and Events* (New York: Grosset and Dunlap, 1940.)

ROBERT W. FOGEL and STANLEY L. ENGERMAN: *Time on the Cross: The Economics of American Negro Slavery* (Boston and Toronto: Little, Brown and Co.; London: Wildwood House, 1974.)

PHILIP S. FONER: *Mark Twain: Social Critic* (New York: International Publishers, 1972.)

EUGENE D. GENOVESE: *Roll, Jordan Roll: The World the Slaves Made* (New York: Pantheon Books, 1974; London: Deutsch, 1975.)

KENNETH M. STAMPP: *The Peculiar Institution: Slavery in the Ante-Bellum South* (New York: Vintage Books; London: Eyre, 1956.)

TONY TANNER: *The Reign of Wonder: Naivety and Reality in American Literature* (London: Cambridge University Press, 1965.)

Money + Freedom

Huck would be free from
father if not for money

Jim + Money — 40 dollars

Money + corruption